"Wealth vs. Worth: Escaping the Luxury Trap"

by

Sid Hiremath

TRAP LIST AND SOLUTIONS

1. **Introduction: What is the Luxury Trap?**
   - Defining the concept of the luxury trap
   - How society equates luxury with success
   - Overview of the psychological, financial, and social impacts

2. **The Psychology of Luxury: Why We Crave More**
   - Understanding the psychology behind luxury consumption
   - The role of status, self-worth, and materialism
   - Instant gratification and emotional satisfaction

3. **Social Media and the Allure of Luxury**
   - How social media amplifies the desire for luxury
   - The rise of influencers and aspirational lifestyles
   - The impact of comparison and FOMO (Fear of Missing Out)

4. **Luxury and Debt: The Financial Cost of the Trap**
   - How luxury spending can lead to financial instability
   - The dangers of lifestyle inflation
   - Case studies on how people fall into debt chasing luxury

5. **Luxury Brands: Selling a Dream**
    - The psychology of luxury marketing
    - How brands create aspirational desires
    - The emotional appeal of luxury advertising

6. **The Social Pressure to Keep Up**
    - Keeping up with peers, colleagues, and society
    - The pressure to conform to luxury standards
    - The personal and emotional toll of trying to fit in

7. **The Hidden Costs of Luxury**
    - Beyond the price tag: time, energy, and mental health costs
    - The emotional exhaustion of maintaining a luxury lifestyle
    - The environmental and social costs of luxury production

8. **Breaking Free from the Luxury Trap**
    - Understanding the difference between needs and wants
    - Developing financial discipline and mindfulness
    - How to build lasting happiness without material excess

9. **Redefining Success: Beyond Material Wealth**
    - How to find personal fulfilment in simplicity
    - The value of experiences over possessions

- Living a life of meaning and authenticity

10. Sustainable Luxury: Is It Possible?

- Can luxury be ethical and sustainable?
- The rise of conscious consumption and ethical brands
- How to enjoy luxury without falling into the trap

11. The Future of Luxury in a Changing World

- The shifting perspectives on luxury in a post-pandemic world
- How technology and minimalism are reshaping luxury
- The evolving definition of success in modern society

12: The Impact of Globalization on Luxury

- **Description:** Explore how globalization has shaped the luxury market, influencing consumer behaviour and brand strategies. Discuss the emergence of luxury markets in developing countries and how cultural shifts affect the perception of luxury.

13: The Role of Authenticity in Luxury Brands

- **Description:** Delve into the importance of authenticity for luxury brands in a market filled with counterfeits and copycats. Discuss how transparency, craftsmanship, and heritage contribute to brand loyalty and consumer trust.

14: Luxury in the Age of Sustainability

- **Description**: Examine the growing trend of sustainability in the luxury industry. Discuss how luxury brands are adopting sustainable practices and how consumers are demanding eco-friendly products, reshaping the definition of luxury.

15: The Psychology of Luxury Shopping

- **Description**: Analyse the psychological factors that drive luxury consumption, including the thrill of the hunt, emotional triggers, and the social dynamics of shopping. Discuss how marketing tactics exploit these psychological factors.

16: The Digital Transformation of Luxury

- **Description**: Investigate how digital technology is transforming the luxury market. Discuss the rise of e-commerce, social media marketing, and virtual experiences, as well as the challenges and opportunities they present.

17: Luxury as a Cultural Statement

- **Description**: Explore how luxury products reflect cultural values and social status. Discuss the role of luxury in shaping identity, community, and social movements.

18: Navigating the Luxury Market Post-Pandemic

- **Description**: Examine the effects of the COVID-19 pandemic on luxury consumption patterns. Discuss how the pandemic has changed consumer priorities and the future of luxury in a post-pandemic world.

19: The Intersection of Technology and Luxury

- **Description**: Discuss how advancements in technology, such as AI and augmented reality, are influencing the luxury market. Explore the implications of technology for personalization, customer experience, and brand engagement.

20: Creating a Balanced Luxury Lifestyle

- **Description**: Offer practical tips and strategies for readers to cultivate a balanced relationship with luxury. Discuss how to enjoy luxury responsibly and align consumption with personal values and well-being.

Conclusion: Finding Balance in a World Obsessed with More

- Reflecting on the lessons learned
- How to balance the desire for luxury with a grounded life
- Final thoughts on escaping the luxury trap

Chapter 1: Introduction: What is the Luxury Trap?

1.1. Defining the Concept of the Luxury Trap

Introduction:
The "Luxury Trap" refers to the relentless pursuit of material wealth, extravagant lifestyles, and high-status symbols in the hope of achieving happiness and success. This chapter delves into the nuances of how luxury, in its modern form, has become synonymous with success, and how it ensnares individuals in a cycle of constant consumption, often leading to emotional, financial, and social consequences.

Detailed Breakdown:

- **What is the Luxury Trap?**
  The luxury trap is a cycle in which individuals continuously seek out luxury, believing that attaining more wealth or status will lead to happiness and fulfilment. However, this cycle often leads to a hollow sense of achievement, where new possessions or experiences lose their allure after a short period, driving the need for more.

- **Why is it a Trap?**
  It's called a "trap" because the pursuit of luxury often leads to emotional burnout, financial strain, and a loss of genuine contentment. People mistakenly believe that luxury equals happiness,

but the constant escalation of desires leaves them feeling unfulfilled.

- **Societal Norms and Expectations:**
  Society glorifies wealth and luxury as markers of success. This is reinforced by media, advertisements, and social media influencers who project an image of the "perfect" life, filled with luxury items. People are conditioned from a young age to associate happiness and success with luxury, creating a psychological attachment to material wealth.

1.2. How Society Equates Luxury with Success

Cultural Influence:
The notion that luxury equals success is deeply ingrained in modern culture. From advertisements to movies, the portrayal of wealthy individuals enjoying life at its finest sets an unrealistic standard for happiness.

Detailed Breakdown:

- **Luxury as a Status Symbol:**
  In many cultures, luxury items like designer clothes, expensive cars, and lavish homes are seen as indicators of personal success. People feel validated when they possess these items, as they symbolize achievement and recognition by society.

- **Influence of social media:**
  Platforms like Instagram, TikTok, and YouTube have amplified the luxury obsession. Influencers flaunt high-end lifestyles, creating a culture of comparison. Regular individuals begin to feel

inadequate if they don't measure up to the luxurious standards set by those they follow.

- **The Psychological Need for Validation:**
  People often seek luxury goods not just for personal satisfaction but also for social validation. The desire to be admired or respected by peers fuels the need to acquire luxury items, leading to a toxic cycle of comparison and competition.

Examples:
Use real-life examples, such as celebrities or influencers, who have perpetuated the luxury ideal. Additionally, case studies of individuals who pursued luxury as a status symbol but faced financial or emotional consequences can add depth to this section.

1.3. Overview of the Psychological, Financial, and Social Impacts

Psychological Impact:
The luxury trap creates a false sense of fulfilment. Psychologically, people believe that buying more will lead to happiness. However, the emotional high of acquiring new luxury goods fades quickly, leaving individuals unsatisfied and craving more.

- **Hedonic Adaptation:**
  This psychological phenomenon refers to the way humans quickly return to a stable level of happiness after a positive or negative event. In the context of luxury, once the thrill of a new purchase wears off, individuals return to their baseline state, prompting them to seek out more luxury items in search of a lasting high.

- **Emotional Consequences:**
  The pursuit of luxury can lead to anxiety, depression, and low self-esteem. Constant comparison with others and the fear of not having enough leads to stress and emotional exhaustion.

Financial Impact:
The luxury trap can have severe financial consequences. People who fall into this cycle often spend beyond their means, accumulating debt to maintain a lavish lifestyle.

- **Debt and Financial Strain:**
  Many people finance their luxury purchases with credit cards or loans, leading to significant debt. As the desire for luxury increases, so does the financial burden.

- **Savings and Investment Sacrifices:**
  Individuals who prioritize luxury often sacrifice long-term financial goals, such as saving for retirement or investing in their future. The focus on immediate gratification leads to poor financial planning.

Social Impact:
The obsession with luxury can lead to strained relationships and social isolation. People caught in the luxury trap may distance themselves from others, either because they feel superior or because they prioritize material possessions over genuine connections.

- **Relationship Strains:**
  Pursuing luxury often leads to conflict in relationships. Partners may disagree on financial priorities, or friends may feel alienated by

someone who constantly seeks to display their wealth.

- **Social Comparison and Envy:**
  Constant comparison with others who appear wealthier or more successful can lead to envy and resentment. This not only harms personal relationships but also fosters a toxic societal environment.

The First Step Toward Understanding the Trap:

Summarize the key points, emphasizing how the luxury trap is not just about material wealth but involves a deeper psychological and social struggle. The chapter sets the tone for the rest of the book by introducing readers to the dangers of equating luxury with success and outlining the broader impacts on personal well-being, finances, and relationships.

Chapter 2: The Psychology of Luxury: Why We Crave More

2.1. Introduction: The Pull of Luxury

This section introduces readers to the psychological allure of luxury, focusing on why humans are inherently drawn to high-status goods and lifestyles. It begins with a compelling scenario or a brief story, showing how even the most frugal individuals can feel tempted by luxury under certain circumstances.

- **Hook:** Start with an example of a luxury brand's marketing campaign (e.g., an iconic watch or designer handbag) and how it creates a sense of desire in viewers. Explain how people who never thought of spending thousands on a handbag suddenly find themselves captivated by the idea.

- **Understanding the Allure:**
  Luxury is not just about having more or better; it's about what these items represent: success, prestige, and social standing. It's also tied to personal identity, self-esteem, and psychological satisfaction.

- **Purpose of the Chapter:**
  Introduce the chapter's focus on uncovering the psychological drives behind luxury consumption, setting the stage for deeper insights into status, self-worth, and the emotional satisfaction that people seek through material goods.

2.2. The Role of Status: Luxury as a Social Symbol

Luxury has long been a social marker of status, power, and prestige. This section delves into how luxury goods and lifestyles are used to signal one's position in society and why people feel compelled to display their status through material means.

- **Social Comparison Theory:**
  People are naturally driven to compare themselves to others. The theory explains how upward comparisons (comparing oneself to those who are better off) drive the desire for luxury. Discuss how these comparisons trigger feelings of envy and the need to "keep up."

- **Veblen Goods and Conspicuous Consumption:**
  Introduce the concept of Veblen goods, named after economist Thorstein Veblen, who coined the term "conspicuous consumption" to describe the act of buying expensive items to display wealth rather than for their practical utility.
  - **Example:** High-end cars, jewellery, or watches that serve more as status symbols than functional tools.
  - **Supporting Data:** Cite studies or statistics showing that people are willing to pay significantly more for luxury brands even when there are functionally equivalent alternatives available.

- **The Desire for Social Recognition:**
  Explain how the human need for recognition, approval, and admiration plays a significant role in the purchase of luxury items. People buy

luxury goods not just for themselves, but to shape how they are perceived by others.

- **Scarcity and Exclusivity:**
  Highlight the psychological power of scarcity. Limited-edition items and exclusive memberships make luxury more desirable. The fewer people who can access something, the more valuable it becomes in the eyes of consumers.

2.3. Luxury and Self-Worth: Do We Define Ourselves by What We Own?

This section examines the connection between luxury and self-worth, exploring how people use luxury goods to shape their identities and feel better about themselves.

- **Materialism and Self-Identity:**
  Materialism is the belief that acquiring possessions is crucial to one's happiness and life satisfaction. People often define themselves by what they own, using luxury to signal personal worth.
  - **Identity Signaling:** Discuss how owning a luxury car or designer bag can be an extension of one's identity. It's not just about buying a product; it's about buying a story and an identity.
- **Luxury as a Coping Mechanism:**
  For some, the pursuit of luxury is a way to cope with low self-esteem, insecurities, or feelings of inadequacy. When people feel unworthy or lesser than their peers, they may turn to luxury goods to "prove" their value.

- - **Psychological Studies**: Refer to research showing the link between low self-esteem and higher levels of materialism. Explain how, paradoxically, buying luxury items may offer a short-term boost in self-worth but ultimately exacerbates insecurities.
- **The Trap of Associating Net Worth with Self-Worth**:
  When individuals start linking their possessions to their personal value, it can create a fragile sense of self. People may become overly dependent on external symbols to define themselves, leading to a continuous need to consume more.

2.4. Instant Gratification and the Search for Emotional Satisfaction (3 pages)

This section covers how luxury consumption provides instant gratification, why the pleasure it brings is fleeting, and how this cycle of temporary satisfaction drives further consumption.

- **The Neuroscience of Luxury Consumption**:
  Explain how luxury purchases activate the brain's reward system. When people buy luxury goods, it triggers the release of dopamine, the "feel-good" neurotransmitter. This surge in pleasure reinforces the behavior, making people want to experience it again and again.
  - **The Instant Gratification Loop**: Discuss how luxury items create a sense of instant pleasure, but how the feeling fades

quickly, leading to a constant search for the next purchase.

- **Emotional Spending:**
  Many people turn to luxury goods as a form of emotional spending — using purchases to cope with stress, anxiety, or even boredom. This behaviour is similar to other forms of addiction, where the object of desire temporarily masks deeper emotional issues.

- **The Hedonic Treadmill:**
  As people accumulate more luxury items, they adapt quickly to the new level of consumption, which means that each new purchase provides less satisfaction than the previous one. This phenomenon, known as the "hedonic treadmill," explains why people can never find lasting happiness in material wealth.

  - **Extended Example:** Use a detailed example of someone who constantly upgrades their car or wardrobe, only to find that each new item feels less satisfying than the last, creating a cycle of perpetual desire.

2.5. The Long-Term Emotional Consequences

The final section discusses how the psychology of luxury consumption, if left unchecked, can lead to long-term emotional consequences, including anxiety, depression, and emptiness.

- **The Emptiness of Materialism:**
  Over time, the emotional highs from luxury

purchases diminish, leaving a void that is often filled with more consumption. This can lead to feelings of emptiness, discontent, and a constant sense of chasing happiness.

- **Emotional Burnout:**
  For those who base their self-worth on luxury, the constant pressure to maintain a high-status lifestyle can lead to emotional burnout, stress, and a diminished sense of life satisfaction.

Conclusion: The True Cost of Craving More

End the chapter by reflecting on the true cost of craving luxury — not in terms of money, but in terms of emotional well-being, personal identity, and relationships. Introduce the next chapter, which will explore how luxury impacts financial decision-making and long-term goals.

Chapter 3: Social Media and the Allure of Luxury

3.1. Introduction: A New Age of Luxury Consumption

In the age of social media, luxury consumption has entered a new phase, where the aspirational lifestyles of the wealthy and famous are accessible to anyone with a smartphone. This section introduces the theme of the chapter by setting up how platforms like Instagram, TikTok, and YouTube have transformed luxury into something that is not only desired but also constantly visible.

- **Hook:** Begin with an anecdote about a viral post showing an influencer's lavish vacation, filled with designer clothes, private jets, and 5-star hotels, followed by thousands of likes and comments admiring the lifestyle.

- **Social media as a Window:** social media has become the modern showroom for luxury brands. It creates a space where everyday users can not only see but also engage with luxury in real time.

- **Purpose of the Chapter:** Introduce the chapter's focus on how social media amplifies the desire for luxury and connects it with social comparison and FOMO.

3.2. The Rise of Influencers and Aspirational Lifestyles

This section delves into the phenomenon of social media influencers and how they've shaped a culture of luxury aspiration. It explains how influencers have become the new ambassadors of luxury, often without traditional celebrity status.

- **Influencers as New Luxury Gatekeepers:**
  Influencers act as modern-day curators of luxury experiences. Through their posts, they create aspirational lifestyles that ordinary people long to emulate.
    - **Example:** Discuss the rise of top influencers who showcase luxury fashion, vacations, and experiences. Platforms like Instagram have allowed everyday people to gain massive followings based on their ability to "live luxuriously."

- **Authenticity vs. Reality:**
  Influencers often present a curated version of reality, where luxury is attainable and normal. This can create a false perception that living such a life is effortless, ignoring the behind-the-scenes sponsorships, debt, or pressure influencers face to maintain this facade.
    - **Supporting Data:** Mention studies that show how people are more likely to believe in influencers' lifestyles than traditional advertisements, leading them to desire the same level of luxury.

- **Luxury as Content:**
  social media turns luxury consumption into content. From unboxing videos to travel vlogs in exotic locations, luxury is no longer just a

product but also a lifestyle performance that audiences can watch, admire, and aspire to.

3.3. The Role of Comparison: How Social Media Fuels Envy

Social media platforms are a breeding ground for social comparison, where users constantly compare their own lives to the glamorous, filtered images of others. This section explores how social media intensifies feelings of inadequacy and desire for luxury.

- **Social Comparison Theory in the Age of Instagram:**
  Social comparison theory suggests that people evaluate their own lives by comparing them to others. Social media amplifies this by providing constant, curated snapshots of luxury that users perceive as reality.
  - **Upward Comparisons:** Focus on how users frequently compare themselves to those better off — wealthier, more stylish, more adventurous — which leads to envy, insecurity, and the desire to "catch up."

- **The Psychology of Envy:**
  Social media envy is particularly strong because the content on these platforms is often designed to highlight the best moments of someone's life. These snapshots of perfection can lead to dissatisfaction with one's own situation.
  - **Example:** Show how following influencers or wealthy friends on social media can lead to feelings of inadequacy and

motivate users to spend beyond their means to emulate the lifestyle they see.

- **Curated Lives, Real Impact**:
  Explain how carefully curated social media posts — luxury vacations, designer clothing, expensive gadgets — can create unrealistic standards, making people feel their lives are lacking in comparison.
    - o **Supporting Data**: Cite research or surveys that demonstrate how social media use correlates with feelings of dissatisfaction, envy, and pressure to purchase luxury items to "keep up" with others.

3.4. FOMO: The Driving Force Behind Luxury Consumption on social media

This section focuses on the role of FOMO (Fear of Missing Out) and how social media exacerbates this phenomenon, pushing people toward luxury consumption as a way to fit in or keep up with their peers.

- **The Power of FOMO**:
  FOMO is the anxiety that others are experiencing something better or more exciting than you are. In the context of luxury, it means feeling like you're missing out on an exclusive experience, product, or lifestyle. Social media intensifies this feeling by constantly showcasing what others are doing and what you're not.
    - o **Example**: Discuss scenarios like seeing posts of exclusive events, luxury launches, or expensive dinners that create a sense

of exclusion for those not participating, leading them to chase after similar experiences.

- **Luxury as the Cure for FOMO:**
  Many people respond to FOMO by purchasing luxury goods or experiences to feel included. They see others enjoying luxury and want to partake in that feeling of belonging.
    - **Supporting Data:** Highlight studies or surveys that link social media use with impulse spending and luxury consumption, driven by FOMO.

- **Scarcity and Exclusivity Amplified by social media:**
  Limited-edition luxury items or events are often showcased on social media, creating a sense of urgency. This drives the fear of missing out, making people feel that if they don't act fast, they'll be left behind.
    - **Example:** Discuss how limited-edition sneaker drops or exclusive designer collaborations are marketed on platforms like Instagram and how users rush to buy these items to avoid missing out.

3.5. The Dark Side of Social Media and Luxury Desire

This section delves into the negative psychological impacts that social media-fueled luxury consumption can have on individuals, such as anxiety, depression, and financial stress.

- **The Psychological Toll of Constant Comparison:**
  social media can create a constant state of

comparison, which can lead to feelings of inadequacy, anxiety, and depression. People may feel that their lives are never good enough because they don't have the luxury items or experiences others flaunt online.

    - **Example:** Include personal accounts or studies that show how excessive social media use has led to decreased self-esteem and increased anxiety, especially among younger users who are more susceptible to social comparison.

- **Financial Strain:**
  The pressure to keep up with luxury trends can lead to financial strain, as people spend beyond their means to maintain a certain lifestyle. This can result in debt, financial insecurity, and long-term consequences.

- **Luxury Addiction:**
  For some, the pursuit of luxury becomes addictive, with social media reinforcing the need for constant upgrades in lifestyle, possessions, and experiences. This can lead to emotional burnout and a never-ending cycle of dissatisfaction.

3.6. Conclusion: Social Media's Influence on the Luxury Trap

Conclude the chapter by summarizing how social media has redefined luxury consumption and exacerbated FOMO and social comparison. Preview the next chapter, which will explore how financial decisions are influenced by the desire for luxury.

Chapter 4: The Financial Impact of Chasing Luxury

This chapter will explore how the pursuit of luxury impacts financial well-being, from overspending and debt accumulation to the broader economic consequences of consumerism driven by luxury aspirations. We'll cover both personal financial implications and the societal trends that emerge from luxury consumption patterns.

4.1. Introduction: Luxury and Personal Finances

Begin the chapter by setting the stage for how the constant chase for luxury can deeply affect personal financial health. This section introduces the concept of overspending to achieve a lifestyle that may not align with one's actual financial means.

- **Hook:** Open with an example of someone who has gone into debt to afford designer goods or luxury vacations, illustrating how common it is to sacrifice financial security for the appearance of wealth.

- **Luxury as a Financial Trap:** Define how luxury becomes not just a symbol of success but a financial burden for many, leading to overspending and living beyond one's means.

- **Purpose of the Chapter:** Explain that this chapter will dissect the financial consequences of luxury consumption, both on an individual level and in a broader societal context.

4.2. The Debt Cycle: How Luxury Can Lead to Financial Ruin

This section focuses on how the desire for luxury can cause people to fall into a cycle of debt and financial strain. It explores the behavioural tendencies that lead individuals to overspend on luxury goods and services, often relying on credit.

- **Living Beyond Your Means:** Many individuals spend more than they earn to keep up with luxury trends, leading to the use of credit cards, loans, or even payday loans to finance their lifestyle.
    - **Example:** Mention how people often buy luxury items on credit, only to later struggle with high-interest debt that spirals out of control.
- **The Debt Trap:**
  Once someone begins using credit to fund luxury purchases, it becomes a slippery slope. Interest payments, late fees, and increasing debt make it harder to maintain financial stability.
    - **Supporting Data:** Cite studies that show how overspending on luxury goods is linked to higher levels of consumer debt, especially among younger generations influenced by social media.

- **Financial Stress:**
  The pursuit of luxury not only causes financial problems but also leads to psychological stress, as people constantly struggle to meet payment deadlines and maintain appearances.
    - **Example:** Discuss the emotional toll that comes from living pay check to pay check while trying to afford luxury items.

4.3. Luxury and Impulse Spending

This section will cover how the luxury industry thrives on impulse purchases, fuelled by marketing tactics, scarcity, and FOMO. We'll explore how these purchases often lead to regret and financial instability.

- **Impulse Buying Psychology:**
  Luxury brands often employ tactics designed to trigger impulse buying, such as limited-time offers, exclusive collaborations, and high-pressure marketing strategies that make consumers feel like they have to act quickly or miss out.
    - **Example:** Discuss how pop-up shops, limited-edition releases, and online sales create a sense of urgency, leading people to make snap decisions that they may later regret.
- **The Power of Marketing:**
  Luxury brands spend billions on advertising that taps into emotions, making consumers feel like they "need" these products to feel successful, attractive, or worthy.

- - **Supporting Data:** Cite research on how targeted advertising and influencer marketing have increased luxury consumption, especially among younger consumers.
- **Post-Purchase Regret:**
  Many people feel an emotional high when buying luxury items, but that feeling can quickly fade, leaving them with regret and a shrinking bank balance.
  - **Example:** Explore how common it is for consumers to regret luxury purchases after the excitement wears off, particularly when those purchases don't match their lifestyle or financial reality.

4.4. The Role of Credit: Financing a Lifestyle

This section delves into how access to credit and financing options has made it easier for people to buy luxury items, often at the cost of long-term financial security.

- **Buy Now, Pay Later:**
  Many luxury brands offer financing options that allow consumers to buy high-end goods without upfront payment. While this makes luxury accessible, it also encourages overspending and leads to long-term debt.
  - **Example:** Explore the growing trend of "buy now, pay later" services and how they contribute to rising consumer debt, especially in the luxury sector.

- **Credit Card Culture:**
  The use of credit cards to fund luxury lifestyles has become normalized, but the high-interest rates associated with these purchases often lead to significant financial consequences.
  - **Supporting Data:** Include statistics on the average credit card debt among luxury consumers and the impact of high-interest rates on long-term financial health.
- **The Illusion of Affordability:**
  Financing options make luxury seem more affordable than it really is, masking the long-term financial strain that comes with these purchases.
  - **Example:** Discuss how payment plans spread out costs, making luxury goods seem attainable, but ultimately lead to financial stress due to compounding interest and fees.

4.5. The Broader Economic Impact of Luxury Consumerism

This section takes a step back to look at the societal and economic consequences of a culture obsessed with luxury. It explores how luxury consumerism drives demand for unsustainable production practices and creates economic inequality.

- **Luxury and Economic Inequality:**
  The luxury industry thrives on exclusivity, and as more people aspire to luxury, the gap between the wealthy and the rest of society grows. This

section discusses how the pursuit of luxury can exacerbate economic inequality and create social divides.

    - **Example:** Discuss how luxury brands cater to the ultra-wealthy, while middle-class consumers struggle to keep up, leading to feelings of inadequacy and increased financial strain.

- **Environmental Impact:**
  The production of luxury goods, especially in the fast fashion and high-tech sectors, has significant environmental consequences. This section explores how luxury consumerism contributes to unsustainable practices that harm the planet.

    - **Supporting Data:** Cite studies that show the environmental impact of luxury goods production, such as the carbon footprint of high-end fashion or the resource extraction needed for luxury electronics.

- **The Shift Towards Ethical Luxury:**
  As consumers become more aware of the economic and environmental costs of luxury, there's a growing trend toward ethical luxury. This section explores how some brands are shifting their business models to focus on sustainability and responsible consumption.

    - **Example:** Highlight brands that are leading the way in ethical luxury, such as those using sustainable materials, fair labour practices, and environmentally friendly production methods.

4.6. Conclusion: Balancing Luxury and Financial Responsibility

Conclude the chapter by summarizing the financial risks of chasing luxury and offering practical advice on how to balance luxury aspirations with financial responsibility. Introduce the next chapter, which will discuss how luxury impacts personal identity and self-worth.

Chapter 5: Luxury Brands: Selling a Dream

This chapter explores how luxury brands craft and sell an aspirational lifestyle, turning their products into symbols of success and desire. It dives into the marketing strategies, emotional appeal, and cultural narratives that luxury brands use to captivate consumers and fuel the dream of a luxurious life.

5.1. The Art of Aspirational Marketing

This section delves into the strategies luxury brands use to create desire, particularly through aspirational marketing.

- **Creating an Ideal:**
  Discuss how luxury brands sell more than just products; they sell an idealized version of life. This section will explain how brands like Gucci, Chanel, and Louis Vuitton associate their products with success, exclusivity, and high social status.
    - **Example:** Describe how advertising campaigns often feature elite lifestyles, exotic locations, and sophisticated people, making the product a symbol of achieving that life.
- **Exclusivity as a Marketing Tool:**
  Examine how scarcity and exclusivity are key tactics in luxury branding. By making their

products hard to obtain, luxury brands increase their perceived value.

- **Example:** Consider how limited-edition items, long waiting lists, or high price points create a sense of privilege and accomplishment when people finally acquire a luxury product.

- **The Emotional Appeal:**
Luxury brands often tap into emotions like aspiration, pride, and even envy. This section explores how emotional storytelling in marketing campaigns makes people feel like they're buying into a dream.

    - **Supporting Data:** Reference studies showing how emotional engagement in advertising significantly increases consumer loyalty and desire for luxury goods.

5.2. Luxury and Lifestyle: The Dream They Sell

Here, we explore how luxury brands link their products to a broader lifestyle that customers aspire to.

- **Luxury as a Lifestyle Choice:**
Luxury brands sell more than just material goods—they promote a lifestyle. This section will discuss how luxury consumption is portrayed as a choice that reflects one's taste, success, and values.

    - **Example:** Brands like Rolex and Hermès don't just sell watches or bags—they promote an exclusive, elite lifestyle, often linked to high-achieving, successful individuals.

- **Aspirational Living:**
  People buy into the dream that owning luxury goods will elevate their lifestyle. Discuss how advertising plays on consumers' desire for a better life, positioning luxury products as the key to unlocking that dream.
    - **Example:** Analyse how luxury car brands like Mercedes-Benz or Aston Martin portray their vehicles as a gateway to prestige, freedom, and sophistication.

- **Celebrity Endorsements and Influence:**
  Celebrities play a significant role in promoting luxury brands by embodying the aspirational lifestyle these brands promise. This section will explain how luxury brands use celebrity endorsements to create an emotional connection between the product and the dream of living like a star.
    - **Example:** Look at how brands like Dior, Versace, and Tiffany use high-profile celebrities or influencers to appeal to consumers' desire to emulate their favourite stars.

5.3. The Power of Storytelling in Luxury Branding

This section delves deeper into how luxury brands use storytelling to create a legacy and craft their dream-like image.

- **Heritage and Craftsmanship:**
  Many luxury brands build their story around a rich heritage and the craftsmanship behind their products. This section will explore how brands use history and tradition to create a sense of authenticity and timeless value.
    - **Example:** Consider how brands like Cartier and Patek Philippe highlight their centuries-old craftsmanship and meticulous attention to detail to justify their high prices and create a sense of legacy.

- **The Brand as a Myth:**
  Luxury brands often turn themselves into cultural myths. This section will explore how they use narrative techniques to make their brand a symbol of success and ultimate achievement.
    - **Example:** Chanel's story as an iconic brand that revolutionized women's fashion, or Louis Vuitton's rise from a Parisian trunk maker to the symbol of global luxury.

- **Storytelling through Experiences:**
  Many luxury brands sell not just a product but an experience. From high-end fashion shows to exclusive launch events, luxury brands use storytelling in every interaction with the consumer.
    - **Example:** Discuss how brands like Burberry or Ralph Lauren create immersive, story-driven experiences for their customers, which go beyond the

product itself and foster emotional connections.

5.4. The Role of Social Media in Amplifying the Dream

Social media has become a powerful platform for luxury brands to spread their dream-like image to a global audience.

- **The Influence of Instagram and Influencers:** social media, particularly platforms like Instagram, has become crucial in amplifying the allure of luxury. This section explores how influencers and celebrities display luxury products to create desire among millions of followers.
    - **Example:** Explain how luxury brands use influencer marketing to portray their products as part of a glamorous, exclusive lifestyle that is within reach but remains just beyond the average consumer's grasp.

- **Curated Perfection:**
Luxury brands carefully curate their social media presence to reflect a flawless, highly desirable lifestyle. This section will analyse how Instagram feeds of luxury brands are designed to evoke perfection, wealth, and exclusivity.
    - **Example:** Review how brands like Prada and Balenciaga use polished, artistic posts to create a sense of aspiration and exclusivity.

- **The Viral Nature of Luxury:**
  Social media's viral nature means that luxury campaigns can spread quickly, creating hype and amplifying the sense of urgency and exclusivity.
  - **Example:** Discuss how limited-edition luxury collaborations, such as Louis Vuitton x Supreme, went viral on social media, creating massive demand and intensifying the allure of luxury.

5.5. The Dream vs. The Reality

This section offers a critical look at the gap between the dream luxury brands sell and the reality of luxury consumption.

- **The Illusion of Luxury:**
  Explore how luxury brands create an illusion of happiness, success, and fulfilments through their products, which may not always align with the reality of consumer satisfaction.
  - **Example:** Discuss how some consumers may experience buyer's remorse or realize that the emotional high of luxury consumption is short-lived.

- **The Psychological Toll:**
  Buying into the luxury dream often leads to financial strain, stress, and a cycle of constant desire. This section discusses the psychological toll on consumers who become trapped in the pursuit of luxury.

- - **Supporting Data**: Cite studies showing that consumers who chase luxury often experience higher levels of anxiety, financial stress, and dissatisfaction.
- **Escaping the Luxury Trap:**
  Conclude the chapter by discussing ways consumers can break free from the luxury trap and find fulfilments in non-material aspects of life.

Chapter 6: The Cost of Luxury: Financial and Emotional Burdens

This chapter explores the hidden costs of luxury, both financially and emotionally. It will dive into how chasing luxury often leads to debt, stress, and dissatisfaction, and how the pressure to maintain a luxurious lifestyle affects individuals' mental health and financial well-being.

6.1. The Financial Strain of Luxury

This section focuses on the financial impact of luxury consumption and the hidden costs of maintaining a luxurious lifestyle.

- **Living Beyond Your Means:**
  Explore how people often go into debt to afford luxury goods, making purchases that exceed their financial capabilities.

    - **Example:** Discuss the rising trend of consumers using credit cards and loans to buy luxury items, leading to long-term financial burdens.

- **The Price of Status:**
  Delve into how luxury goods are not just expensive but are often purchased for the status they provide, and how maintaining this status becomes a costly endeavour.

- o **Example:** Explain how luxury brands like Rolex and Cartier target individuals seeking to maintain or elevate their social standing, causing them to overspend on status symbols.
- **The Trap of Upgrading:**
  Discuss how consumers who start buying luxury often feel the need to continuously upgrade to newer, more expensive items to maintain the appearance of wealth.
  - o **Example:** Look at how people frequently upgrade their luxury cars, gadgets, or fashion accessories, leading to a cycle of never-ending expenditure.

6.2. Emotional and Psychological Costs

This section addresses the emotional toll that luxury consumption can have on individuals.

- **Luxury and Self-Worth:**
  Explain how people often tie their self-worth to the luxury items they own, creating emotional dependence on material possessions.
  - o **Example:** Explore how luxury buyers may feel inadequate or unworthy without the latest products, causing emotional strain and insecurity.
- **The Anxiety of Keeping Up:**
  Discuss how the pressure to keep up with others' luxury lifestyles, often amplified by social media, leads to stress, anxiety, and feelings of inadequacy.

- **Supporting Data:** Include studies that show how constantly comparing oneself to others on social media, particularly regarding luxury lifestyles, can lead to mental health issues like depression and anxiety.

- **The Cycle of Discontent:**
Examine how luxury goods often fail to provide lasting happiness or fulfilments, leading to a continuous cycle of dissatisfaction and craving for more.
  - **Example:** Analyse how consumers frequently experience buyer's remorse after making luxury purchases and how the temporary emotional boost fades quickly, creating a need for the next purchase.

6.3. The Social Pressure to Consume Luxury

This section covers the societal expectations and social pressure that drive individuals toward luxury consumption.

- **The Fear of Being Left Behind:**
Explore how social pressures, particularly from peers and social media, drive people to pursue luxury goods to avoid feeling left out or inferior.
  - **Example:** Discuss how certain social circles promote luxury consumption as a measure of success, making it difficult for individuals to resist the pressure.

- **Keeping Up with Appearances:**
Examine how societal expectations push people

to maintain a luxurious lifestyle, even when it leads to financial strain or personal unhappiness.

- o **Example:** Consider how people feel pressured to wear designer clothes or drive expensive cars to fit into certain social groups or professional environments.

- **The Role of social media:**
Social media plays a huge role in amplifying societal pressure to consume luxury. Discuss how platforms like Instagram and Facebook turn luxury consumption into a public display of status and wealth, encouraging more people to join the race.

  - o **Example:** Explore how influencers and celebrities fuel the pressure by flaunting their luxury lifestyles, creating a sense of inadequacy among followers who can't keep up.

6.4. The Hidden Costs of Maintaining a Luxury Lifestyle

This section focuses on the often overlooked, ongoing expenses of owning luxury items.

- **Maintenance and Upkeep:**
Luxury items are expensive to maintain, whether it's a high-end car, a designer watch, or a luxury home. Explore how the maintenance costs of luxury possessions can add up, leading to more financial strain.

  - o **Example:** Discuss how maintaining a luxury car, such as a Ferrari or Porsche, requires costly servicing, insurance, and repairs that go beyond the initial purchase price.

- **Lifestyle Inflation:**
Once individuals start buying luxury, their overall lifestyle tends to inflate, leading to increased expenses in other areas, such as dining, travel, and entertainment.
    - **Example:** Analyse how individuals who purchase luxury goods often feel the need to upgrade other aspects of their lives, such as dining at expensive restaurants or taking luxury vacations, to match their new image.

- **Social Expectations of Luxury Owners:**
Explore how people who own luxury items are often expected to participate in expensive social activities, adding to the hidden costs of their lifestyle.
    - **Example:** Discuss how owning a luxury car or home can lead to invitations to exclusive events or high-end social circles, which come with their own financial obligations.

6.5. Escaping the Financial and Emotional Burdens of Luxury

This section offers practical advice for individuals who want to escape the financial and emotional burdens of luxury consumption.

- **Finding Fulfilment Beyond Materialism:**
Explore alternative ways of finding happiness and

self-worth that don't involve luxury goods, such as cultivating relationships, experiences, and personal growth.
    - **Example:** Discuss how people who focus on personal achievements, hobbies, or experiences often find more lasting fulfilment than those who rely on material possessions.
- **Budgeting and Financial Planning:**
Offer strategies for creating a sustainable budget that prioritizes long-term financial health over luxury spending.
    - **Example:** Provide tips on how to avoid impulse luxury purchases and focus on saving for more meaningful investments, such as education, travel, or retirement.
- **Breaking the Cycle of Comparison:**
Discuss ways to avoid the social pressures that lead to luxury consumption, such as limiting social media exposure, setting personal goals, and redefining success on your own terms.
    - **Example:** Share stories of individuals who have successfully stepped away from luxury consumption and found happiness in simplicity and contentment.

Chapter 7: The Hidden Costs of Luxury

In this chapter, we explore the often-overlooked consequences of luxury consumption. While luxury items are marketed as symbols of success and sophistication, there are hidden costs—both personal and societal—that come with the pursuit of luxury.

7.1. The Financial Burden of Luxury

Luxury goods come at a high price, and often, consumers sacrifice financial stability for the allure of prestige.

- **Debt and Over-Spending:**
  Many consumers are willing to take on debt to afford luxury items, leading to long-term financial strain.
    - **Example:** Discuss how credit cards and instalment plans have made it easier for individuals to purchase luxury goods without considering the financial burden.
- **Opportunity Cost:**
  When individuals spend large sums on luxury goods, they forgo other opportunities, such as investing in education, savings, or long-term assets.
    - **Example:** Explore how purchasing luxury cars or watches might prevent someone

from investing in real estate or their retirement funds.

7.2. The Environmental Impact of Luxury

Luxury items are often marketed as eco-friendly or sustainable, but the reality is that the luxury industry has a significant environmental footprint.

- **Resource Extraction:**
  The production of luxury goods often involves the extraction of rare materials, which can contribute to environmental degradation.
    - **Example:** Examine the impact of luxury goods made from rare leathers, exotic woods, or precious metals on biodiversity and ecosystems.

- **High Carbon Footprint:**
  The luxury fashion industry, in particular, is responsible for significant greenhouse gas emissions due to complex supply chains, global transportation, and manufacturing processes.
    - **Example:** Analyse how the production and transportation of luxury goods, such as high-end clothing and accessories, contribute to global carbon emissions.

- **Waste and Overproduction:**
  Luxury brands sometimes destroy unsold goods to maintain exclusivity, leading to waste and unnecessary environmental harm.
    - **Example:** Discuss the controversy surrounding brands like Burberry, which

were reported to burn unsold inventory to avoid discounting or devaluing their products.

7.3. The Social Costs of Luxury

The obsession with luxury can create social inequalities and exacerbate feelings of inadequacy among those who cannot afford such items.

- **Social Division:**
  Luxury consumption can deepen social divides by creating a clear distinction between those who can afford luxury goods and those who cannot, perpetuating classism.
    - **Example:** Look at how the visibility of luxury items on social media can reinforce socioeconomic disparities and make lower-income individuals feel excluded.

- **Mental Health and Status Anxiety:**
  The constant pursuit of luxury and status can lead to mental health issues such as anxiety, depression, and low self-esteem.
    - **Example:** Discuss how the pressure to keep up with luxury trends can create stress and anxiety, especially for younger generations who are influenced by social media.

- **Materialism vs. Relationships:**
  The focus on acquiring luxury goods can shift priorities away from meaningful relationships,

causing emotional isolation and strained connections with others.

- **Example:** Explore how individuals who prioritize luxury consumption may neglect personal relationships, leading to a sense of emptiness despite their material success.

7.4. Ethical Considerations in the Luxury Industry

While luxury brands often tout craftsmanship and quality, the industry has faced criticism for questionable labour practices and ethical concerns.

- **Exploitation of Labor:**
  Despite the high cost of luxury goods, workers in supply chains are often underpaid and subjected to poor working conditions.
  - **Example:** Investigate the production of luxury handbags or shoes, where labour may be outsourced to countries with lower wages and lax labour laws.

- **Animal Cruelty:**
  Many luxury goods are made from animal-derived materials, such as fur, leather, and exotic skins, raising concerns about animal rights and ethical sourcing.
  - **Example:** Analyse how luxury brands like Hermès and Louis Vuitton have faced criticism for their use of animal products, leading to calls for cruelty-free alternatives.

- **Greenwashing:**
  Some luxury brands market themselves as environmentally responsible, but their actual practices may not align with their claims, leading to accusations of greenwashing.
    - **Example:** Discuss how some luxury brands promote limited sustainable collections while continuing unsustainable practices in other parts of their production process.

7.5. The Psychological Trap of Luxury

The psychological allure of luxury can trap consumers in a never-ending cycle of consumption, where the pursuit of more becomes insatiable.

- **Hedonic Treadmill:**
  The concept of the hedonic treadmill suggests that as people acquire luxury items, their level of satisfaction increases only temporarily before returning to a baseline, prompting them to seek more.
    - **Example:** Examine how individuals who purchase luxury goods often find themselves desiring newer, more expensive items, creating a cycle of dissatisfaction.
- **Self-Worth and Luxury:**
  For many, luxury becomes tied to self-worth, where owning high-end products serves as a measure of personal value and success.

- **Example:** Explore the psychological impact of linking one's identity to material possessions, and how this can lead to low self-esteem if one cannot keep up with luxury consumption.

- **Fear of Missing Out (FOMO) and Luxury:** Social media and influencer culture have amplified the fear of missing out on luxury experiences and products, pushing consumers to make impulsive, high-cost purchases.

  - **Example:** Look at how luxury brands capitalize on FOMO through limited releases and exclusive collections, driving up demand and creating urgency to purchase.

Chapter 8: Breaking Free from the Luxury Trap

In this chapter, we delve into the strategies and mindsets required to break free from the psychological, financial, and social pressures of luxury consumption. By understanding and applying these concepts, individuals can pursue a more authentic and fulfilling life that is not dictated by materialistic values.

8.1. Redefining Success and Happiness

The conventional notion of success often intertwines with the accumulation of luxury goods, leading individuals to equate material wealth with personal worth. Breaking free from this mindset begins with redefining what success and happiness mean.

- **Shifting from Material to Experiential:** Research indicates that experiences, such as travel, education, or quality time with loved ones, bring more enduring happiness than luxury items. Understanding this can help individuals prioritize experiences over possessions.
    - **Example:** Share findings from psychological studies that illustrate how experiences contribute to a greater sense of well-being compared to material possessions.
- **Contentment and Minimalism:** Embracing minimalism encourages individuals to

focus on what truly matters, fostering a sense of contentment by reducing attachment to luxury and material wealth.

  - **Example:** Narrate stories of individuals who adopted minimalism and discovered a renewed sense of joy and fulfilment through fewer, more meaningful possessions.

- **Reevaluating Personal Goals:**
  Encourage readers to reflect on their goals and consider whether they stem from societal expectations or personal values. Aiming for personal growth, self-improvement, and meaningful relationships can lead to more genuine happiness.

  - **Exercise:** Provide prompts for self-reflection that help readers explore their values and reimagine their definitions of success.

8.2. Financial Discipline: Prioritizing Long-Term Wealth

Financial discipline is a cornerstone of escaping the luxury trap. Developing a strong financial foundation allows individuals to prioritize long-term stability over immediate gratification.

- **Creating a Financial Plan:**
  Encourage readers to create a budget that prioritizes savings and investments over luxury expenditures. Discuss how budgeting helps manage finances effectively.

- - **Example:** Provide a simple budgeting template and examples of how to allocate funds for necessities, savings, and discretionary spending.

- **Wealth vs. Status:**
  Emphasize the difference between perceived wealth (showing off luxury items) and actual wealth (financial independence). Understanding this distinction helps individuals recognize that true wealth doesn't require luxury consumption.
  - **Example:** Share success stories of individuals who found financial freedom through smart investing rather than indulging in luxury spending.

- **Building an Emergency Fund:**
  Discuss the importance of having an emergency fund as a buffer against financial instability. This approach promotes peace of mind, reducing the impulse to splurge on luxury items during stressful times.
  - **Actionable Tip:** Suggest steps to build an emergency fund, starting with small, manageable contributions.

8.3. Emotional Intelligence and Mindfulness

Recognizing emotional triggers and cultivating mindfulness can significantly reduce the urge to seek luxury as a means of validation or emotional comfort.

- **Identifying Emotional Triggers:**
  Many luxury purchases are often made in

response to feelings such as stress, boredom, or low self-esteem. Identifying these triggers can help individuals understand their motivations for consumption.

  - **Example:** Present scenarios that illustrate common emotional triggers and how they lead to impulsive luxury purchases.

- **Developing Emotional Resilience:** Encourage readers to cultivate emotional resilience by finding healthier coping mechanisms, such as exercising, meditating, or engaging in creative activities.

  - **Exercise:** Provide mindfulness techniques that can help individuals manage their emotions without resorting to luxury purchases.

- **Mindful Consumption:** Advocate for a mindful approach to consumption, where individuals pause to assess whether a luxury item truly enhances their lives or fulfils deeper emotional needs.

  - **Example:** Share stories of people who practiced mindful spending and how it transformed their approach to luxury consumption.

8.4. Disconnecting from Social Media Influence

Social media plays a significant role in fostering desires for luxury. By managing social media consumption, individuals can counteract the influence of materialism.

- **Curating a Positive Feed:**
  Encourage readers to curate their social media feeds by following accounts that promote personal development, sustainability, and mindfulness instead of luxury-focused influencers.
  - **Example:** Provide a list of recommended accounts or hashtags that align with healthier values.
- **Practicing Digital Detox:**
  Suggest regular breaks from social media to reconnect with reality and focus on personal goals rather than materialistic aspirations.
  - **Example:** Outline steps for a digital detox, including duration, activities to engage in during the break, and how to re-enter social media mindfully.

8.5. Building a Value-Driven Life

Ultimately, breaking free from the luxury trap requires a commitment to living according to one's values rather than societal pressures. This involves embracing a life focused on relationships, personal growth, and meaningful contributions.

- **Living with Purpose:**
  Emphasize that individuals who align their actions with their core values are less likely to feel the need for luxury goods, as they derive fulfilment from meaningful pursuits.

- **Example:** Highlight stories of individuals who have transitioned from materialistic lifestyles to purpose-driven living and the positive impact on their happiness.

- **Practicing Gratitude:**
  Cultivating gratitude can shift focus from what one lacks to appreciating what one has, reducing the desire for luxury consumption.
  - **Exercise:** Suggest daily gratitude practices, such as journaling or sharing gratitude with friends and family, to foster a more positive mindset.

Chapter 9: Redefining Success: Beyond Material Wealth

In this chapter, we will explore the concept of success beyond material wealth, emphasizing the importance of defining personal success in ways that align with one's values and aspirations. By understanding that true fulfilment comes from various dimensions of life, individuals can escape the constraints of materialism and pursue a more meaningful existence.

9.1. Understanding Traditional Success Metrics

Society often equates success with wealth, luxury, and status, leading to a narrow understanding of what it means to be successful.

- **Cultural Definitions of Success:**
  Discuss how different cultures define success and the role that wealth plays in these definitions. Emphasize the impact of cultural narratives on individual aspirations.

    o **Example:** Share stories from different cultures that illustrate varying definitions of success, such as community contribution, artistic achievement, or family well-being.

- **Critique of Materialism:**
  Analyse the drawbacks of equating success solely with material wealth, including stress, dissatisfaction, and the fleeting nature of luxury.

- **Example:** Use case studies of successful individuals who found themselves unfulfilled despite financial success to illustrate this point.

9.2. The Shift Toward Holistic Success

The concept of holistic success encompasses multiple facets of life, including emotional, spiritual, and relational aspects, rather than focusing exclusively on material wealth.

- **Defining Holistic Success:**
  Present a comprehensive definition of success that includes emotional well-being, healthy relationships, personal growth, and community contribution.
  - **Example:** Introduce frameworks or models that illustrate how different areas of life contribute to overall success and fulfilment.

- **Value of Emotional Well-Being:**
  Discuss the significance of mental health and emotional intelligence as vital components of success, highlighting how they contribute to resilience and life satisfaction.
  - **Exercise:** Provide a self-assessment tool for readers to evaluate their emotional well-being and identify areas for improvement.

9.3. Personal Values and Success

Aligning personal values with one's definition of success can lead to greater fulfilment and authenticity.

- **Identifying Core Values:**
  Guide readers through a process of identifying their core values and understanding how these values shape their aspirations and definition of success.
    - **Exercise:** Offer a step-by-step activity to help readers articulate their values and reflect on how they influence their goals.

- **Creating a Personal Success Plan:**
  Encourage readers to develop a personal success plan that integrates their values, aspirations, and holistic definitions of success.
    - **Example:** Share templates or models for creating a success plan, including specific goals related to various life dimensions.

9.4. The Role of Community and Relationships

Success is often amplified through meaningful connections and contributions to community, emphasizing that individual achievements should not be isolated.

- **Importance of Relationships:**
  Discuss how nurturing relationships and connections contributes to a deeper sense of success, offering support, joy, and shared experiences.

- **Example**: Highlight stories of individuals who found fulfilment through community involvement and building meaningful relationships rather than solely pursuing personal wealth.

- **Contribution to Society**:
  Explore the concept of success as a contribution to society, showcasing how giving back and making a difference can lead to a more fulfilling life.
  - **Case Study**: Present examples of successful individuals who prioritize social impact and community service in their definitions of success.

9.5. Embracing Lifelong Learning and Growth

Focusing on personal development and lifelong learning fosters a sense of achievement that transcends material wealth.

- **Growth Mindset**:
  Introduce the concept of a growth mindset, which encourages individuals to view challenges and failures as opportunities for learning and improvement.
  - **Example**: Share anecdotes of individuals who achieved personal growth through overcoming obstacles and pursuing lifelong learning.

- **Pursuing Passions**:
  Encourage readers to engage in activities that

ignite their passions and interests, reinforcing that success can also come from personal satisfaction and fulfilment.

- **Actionable Tips:** Provide suggestions for readers to explore hobbies, education, and personal projects that resonate with their interests.

Chapter 10: Sustainable Luxury: Is It Possible?

In this chapter, we explore the intersection of luxury and sustainability, questioning whether the two can coexist in a world increasingly concerned with environmental and ethical considerations. As consumer awareness grows, the luxury industry is challenged to adapt and redefine itself in ways that are both luxurious and sustainable.

10.1. Defining Sustainable Luxury

To understand whether sustainable luxury is achievable, we first need to define what constitutes both "sustainability" and "luxury."

- **What is Sustainability?**
  Discuss the principles of sustainability, including environmental, social, and economic dimensions, and how they relate to consumer goods.

    - **Example:** Present definitions and frameworks, such as the United Nations Sustainable Development Goals (SDGs), to contextualize sustainability within the luxury sector.

- **Understanding Luxury:**
  Define luxury beyond just high price tags, focusing on exclusivity, craftsmanship, heritage, and emotional resonance.

- - **Example:** Compare and contrast traditional luxury brands with emerging brands that prioritize sustainable practices.
- **Consumer Perceptions:**
  Examine how consumer perceptions of luxury are evolving with the growing emphasis on sustainability, shifting from purely materialistic views to values-based definitions.

10.2. The Luxury Industry's Environmental Footprint

Examine the ecological impact of the luxury industry, highlighting the environmental challenges associated with luxury goods.

- **Resource Intensity:**
  Discuss the resource-intensive nature of luxury production, including the use of raw materials, energy consumption, and waste generation.
  - **Case Study:** Provide statistics or examples of the environmental impacts of high-fashion brands, including water pollution and carbon emissions.
- **Supply Chain Challenges:**
  Explore the complexities of luxury supply chains, from sourcing rare materials to ensuring ethical labour practices.
  - **Example:** Analyse the challenges faced by luxury brands in managing their supply chains sustainably, and the repercussions of failing to do so.

- **Consumer Behaviour:**
  Analyse how consumer behaviour influences the luxury market and its sustainability practices, including trends toward fast fashion and excessive consumption.
    - **Example:** Highlight research showing consumer preferences for sustainable products and the rise of eco-conscious luxury brands.

10.3. The Rise of Sustainable Luxury Brands

Explore how luxury brands are beginning to embrace sustainability, offering insights into successful case studies.

- **Innovative Practices:**
  Discuss brands that have integrated sustainable practices into their business models, such as ethical sourcing, biodegradable materials, and eco-friendly production processes.
    - **Example:** Highlight brands like Stella McCartney and Patagonia that are leading the charge in sustainable luxury, showcasing their initiatives and impact.

- **Transparency and Ethical Production:**
  Examine the growing importance of transparency in luxury production and how consumers are demanding accountability from brands regarding their sustainability practices.
    - **Case Study:** Present brands that have adopted traceability in their supply chains

and how this contributes to consumer trust.

- **Luxury and Craftsmanship:**
Explore the relationship between craftsmanship and sustainability, emphasizing how high-quality, durable products can reduce waste and promote responsible consumption.
    - **Example:** Feature artisans and luxury brands that prioritize craftsmanship, showcasing their commitment to sustainable materials and practices.

10.4. Consumer Responsibility and Awareness

As the luxury industry evolves, consumers play a crucial role in driving the demand for sustainable practices.

- **Empowering Consumers:**
Encourage readers to educate themselves about the sustainability practices of luxury brands and the environmental implications of their purchases.
    - **Actionable Steps:** Provide tips on how consumers can research brands, such as looking for certifications, ethical labels, and company sustainability reports.

- **Conscious Consumption:**
Advocate for a shift towards conscious consumption, urging readers to prioritize quality over quantity and consider the long-term value of their purchases.

- **Exercise**: Suggest creating a checklist for consumers to evaluate the sustainability of luxury products before making a purchase.

- **Social Media's Role**:
  Discuss the influence of social media in promoting sustainable luxury and how consumers can leverage these platforms to hold brands accountable.
  - **Case Study**: Highlight campaigns that have successfully raised awareness about sustainable luxury, encouraging consumers to participate actively.

10.5. The Future of Sustainable Luxury

Looking ahead, we consider the potential trajectory of the luxury industry and its relationship with sustainability.

- **Challenges and Opportunities**:
  Discuss the challenges that luxury brands face in implementing sustainable practices while maintaining their core identity.
  - **Example**: Explore potential conflicts between luxury's inherent exclusivity and the inclusivity of sustainability efforts.

- **Vision for the Future**:
  Envision a future where luxury and sustainability are seamlessly integrated, inspiring readers to advocate for and support brands that align with these values.

- **Case Study:** Present visionary brands or initiatives that exemplify the future of sustainable luxury.

10.6. Innovations in Sustainable Luxury

Discuss the innovations that are shaping the future of luxury with a focus on sustainability.

- **Technological Advancements:**
  Highlight how technology is enabling brands to adopt sustainable practices, such as 3D printing, sustainable materials, and digital platforms for sharing resources.
  - **Example:** Showcase brands using blockchain technology to enhance transparency and traceability in their supply chains.

- **Circular Economy in Luxury:**
  Explore the concept of the circular economy and how luxury brands are adapting their business models to promote recycling, upcycling, and responsible disposal.
  - **Case Study:** Feature brands that have successfully implemented circular economy principles, such as garment rental services and recycling programs.

Chapter 11: The Future of Luxury in a Changing World

As we move into an era characterized by rapid change and evolving consumer values, the landscape of luxury is set to undergo significant transformations. This chapter explores the future of luxury consumption, considering the shifts in societal expectations, technological advancements, and the increasing emphasis on sustainability and authenticity. We will discuss how these factors are reshaping the definition of luxury and what it means to consumers in a changing world.

11.1. Evolving Consumer Values

Analyse how changing consumer values are influencing the luxury market, shifting the focus from material possessions to experiences and emotional connections.

- **Experience over Possessions:**
  Discuss the trend of valuing experiences over material goods, particularly among younger consumers. This shift suggests a movement away from traditional luxury items towards memorable experiences.

    - **Example:** Explore how luxury brands are adapting by offering exclusive experiences, such as personalized travel or unique events.

- **Authenticity and Transparency:**
  Examine the growing demand for authenticity in

luxury brands. Consumers today are more informed and seek brands that align with their values.

- **Case Study**: Highlight brands that have successfully communicated their authentic stories and built trust with consumers.

11.2. The Rise of Sustainability

Investigate the increasing importance of sustainability in luxury consumption, as consumers demand eco-friendly practices from brands.

- **Sustainable Practices:**
  Discuss how luxury brands are integrating sustainable materials and practices into their production processes. This includes using eco-friendly materials, reducing waste, and promoting ethical sourcing.
  - **Example**: Present case studies of luxury brands that have made significant strides toward sustainability and their impact on the environment.

- **Consumer Expectations:**
  Explore how consumers are holding brands accountable for their environmental impact, demanding transparency in sustainability efforts.
  - **Actionable Steps**: Suggest how consumers can support sustainable luxury brands and make informed choices.

11.3. Technological Innovations and Luxury

Examine the role of technology in shaping the future of luxury consumption, from e-commerce to augmented reality.

- **E-Commerce and Digital Experiences:** Analyse how luxury brands are embracing e-commerce platforms and digital marketing to reach a wider audience. The convenience of online shopping is becoming increasingly appealing to consumers.
    - **Example:** Discuss innovative online shopping experiences that enhance customer engagement, such as virtual showrooms or personalized recommendations.
- **Augmented Reality and Virtual Reality:** Explore the impact of AR and VR technologies on luxury marketing and consumer experiences, allowing customers to visualize products in their own environments or try them virtually.
    - **Case Study:** Highlight brands that have successfully implemented AR/VR strategies to enhance customer experiences and drive sales.

11.4. The Influence of Social Media

Investigate the ongoing influence of social media on luxury consumption, emphasizing how platforms shape brand perceptions and consumer desires.

- **Social Media as a Marketing Tool:**
  Discuss the role of social media in promoting luxury brands, particularly through influencer partnerships and user-generated content.
    - **Case Study:** Highlight successful social media campaigns that have elevated luxury brands' visibility and desirability.

- **Building Communities:**
  Explore how luxury brands can leverage social media to build engaged communities around their products, fostering loyalty and connection among consumers.
    - **Example:** Present brands that have cultivated strong online communities through interactive content and engagement strategies.

11.5. Challenges Facing Luxury Brands

Address the challenges luxury brands will face in the future, including economic fluctuations, shifting consumer preferences, and competition from emerging markets.

- **Economic Sensitivity:**
  Analyse how luxury brands are affected by economic downturns and changing consumer spending habits. The luxury market is often seen as resilient, but economic factors can significantly influence purchasing behaviour.

- **Case Study:** Examine how luxury brands adapted during economic recessions and their strategies for recovery.

- **Competition from Emerging Markets:**
  Discuss the rise of luxury consumption in emerging markets and the challenges traditional luxury brands may face as new players enter the market.

  - **Actionable Steps:** Suggest how established luxury brands can innovate and adapt to maintain their competitive edge.

11.6. Reimagining Luxury for the Future

Conclude with reflections on what luxury will look like in the future, emphasizing the importance of adaptability and innovation.

- **A Holistic Approach:**
  Emphasize that the future of luxury will require brands to adopt a holistic approach, integrating sustainability, technology, and authentic storytelling to resonate with consumers.

- **A New Definition of Luxury:**
  Propose a new definition of luxury that prioritizes experiences, emotional connections, and social responsibility over mere material wealth.

Chapter 12: The Future of Luxury in a Changing World

Introduction

The luxury market is in a state of flux, influenced by various factors ranging from changing consumer behaviours to global economic shifts. As we move into a new era characterized by rapid technological advancements, increasing awareness of social and environmental issues, and the rise of diverse consumer demographics, the future of luxury presents both opportunities and challenges. This chapter explores the evolving landscape of luxury, examining key trends and projections that will shape the future of luxury brands.

1. The Impact of Technology on Luxury

The advent of new technologies is transforming the luxury industry in unprecedented ways. From e-commerce to virtual reality, technology is reshaping how consumers interact with brands and how brands deliver their products and services.

- **E-Commerce Revolution:** The pandemic accelerated the shift towards online shopping, and luxury brands are increasingly investing in their e-commerce platforms. The convenience of online shopping, coupled with advanced logistics, allows consumers to access luxury products from anywhere in the world. Brands that prioritize their digital presence and offer seamless online experiences are likely to thrive in this new landscape.

- **Augmented Reality (AR) and Virtual Reality (VR):** AR and VR technologies are creating immersive shopping experiences that allow consumers to engage with products in innovative ways. For instance, luxury fashion brands are using AR to enable customers to virtually try on clothes or accessories before making a purchase. This technology not only enhances the shopping experience but also reduces return rates, a significant concern for online retailers.

- **Personalization through Data Analytics:** Brands are leveraging data analytics to understand consumer preferences and behaviours better. By analysing customer data, luxury brands can offer personalized recommendations and tailored marketing campaigns. This level of personalization fosters deeper connections with consumers and enhances brand loyalty.

2. Sustainability as a Core Value

As awareness of environmental issues grows, sustainability is becoming a core value for luxury consumers. The future of luxury will be defined by brands that prioritize ethical practices and sustainable sourcing.

- **Eco-Friendly Materials:** Luxury brands are increasingly adopting eco-friendly materials in their products. From organic cotton to recycled plastics, the use of sustainable materials not only appeals to environmentally conscious consumers but also positions brands as leaders in the sustainability movement.

- **Transparent Supply Chains:** Consumers are demanding transparency in the supply chain. Brands that openly communicate their sourcing and manufacturing processes build trust and credibility. For example, luxury brands are increasingly sharing information about the origins of their materials and the labour conditions of their workers.

- **Circular Economy Initiatives:** The concept of a circular economy—where products are designed for reuse, repair, and recycling—is gaining traction in the luxury sector. Brands are launching initiatives that promote product longevity and encourage consumers to return used items for recycling or resale. This approach not only reduces waste but also aligns with consumer values.

3. The Rise of Conscious Consumerism

The future of luxury will be shaped by conscious consumerism, where individuals prioritize their values over material possessions. This shift is influencing how luxury brands approach their marketing strategies and product offerings.

- **Experience Over Ownership:** Modern luxury consumers are increasingly valuing experiences over material possessions. Instead of purchasing luxury items, consumers are opting for unique experiences, such as luxury travel, fine dining, and exclusive events. Brands that offer experiential luxury—where the focus is on creating memorable moments—are likely to resonate with this new generation of consumers.

- **Social Responsibility**: Luxury brands are being held accountable for their social impact. Consumers are demanding that brands take a stand on social issues and contribute to positive change. Brands that actively engage in social responsibility initiatives, such as supporting local communities or advocating for equality, will build stronger connections with consumers.

- **Community Building**: The future of luxury will involve building communities around shared values. Brands that foster a sense of belonging and create platforms for consumers to connect with each other will differentiate themselves in a crowded marketplace. This community-driven approach enhances brand loyalty and creates a more profound emotional connection with consumers.

4. The Evolution of Luxury Definitions

The traditional definitions of luxury—characterized solely by exclusivity and high price points—are evolving. The future of luxury will be more inclusive and diverse, reflecting the changing values of consumers.

- **Diversity and Inclusivity**: Luxury brands are recognizing the importance of diversity and inclusivity in their marketing and product offerings. Brands that embrace diverse models, representations, and narratives resonate with a broader audience. This shift toward inclusivity not only reflects societal changes but also taps into the aspirations of a diverse consumer base.

- **Local and Artisanal Luxury**: As consumers seek authenticity, there is a growing appreciation for local and artisanal luxury. Brands that celebrate craftsmanship, heritage, and local culture stand out in a globalized market. This trend allows consumers to connect with unique products that tell a story and reflect their values.

- **Redefining Status Symbols:** The concept of status is evolving. Modern consumers are moving away from traditional symbols of wealth, such as designer logos, towards more subtle markers of success, such as sustainable practices and meaningful experiences. Brands that adapt to this shift will remain relevant in the future luxury landscape.

5. Global Market Dynamics

The luxury market is increasingly influenced by global economic dynamics and geopolitical factors. Understanding these trends is crucial for brands seeking to navigate the complexities of the global luxury landscape.

- **Emerging Markets:** As emerging markets continue to grow, luxury brands are expanding their presence in regions like Asia, Africa, and Latin America. These markets present significant growth opportunities, but brands must navigate cultural differences and local regulations to succeed.

- **Geopolitical Factors:** Political and economic instability can impact luxury consumption. Brands must remain agile and responsive to changing geopolitical landscapes, adapting their strategies to mitigate risks and capitalize on emerging opportunities.

- **Global Consumer Trends**: Luxury brands need to stay attuned to global consumer trends, including shifts in demographics, lifestyle preferences, and cultural influences. This understanding allows brands to anticipate market changes and tailor their offerings to meet evolving consumer demands.

6. The Future of Retail: Omnichannel Experiences

The future of retail will be characterized by omnichannel experiences, where consumers can seamlessly transition between online and offline shopping. This approach is essential for luxury brands seeking to provide a holistic customer experience.

- **Physical Retail Spaces**: While e-commerce is on the rise, physical retail spaces remain essential for luxury brands. Flagship stores and experiential boutiques offer consumers a chance to engage with the brand on a personal level. These spaces serve as platforms for storytelling, showcasing craftsmanship, and building emotional connections.

- **Integrated Online and Offline Experiences**: Luxury brands must create integrated online and offline experiences that allow consumers to interact with the brand in multiple ways. For example, a consumer may browse a product online, visit a store for a fitting, and complete the purchase through a mobile app. This seamless experience enhances convenience and customer satisfaction.

- **Technology-Enhanced Retail**: The integration of technology in retail spaces will continue to evolve. From interactive displays to personalized service through AI-driven tools, technology will enhance the in-store experience. Brands that leverage technology to create unique, engaging shopping environments will capture the attention of consumers.

7. Conclusion: A New Era of Luxury

The future of luxury is characterized by transformation and adaptation. As consumers' values evolve, luxury brands must respond by embracing sustainability, inclusivity, and conscious consumerism. The impact of technology and globalization will continue to reshape the luxury landscape, offering both challenges and opportunities.

In this new era, luxury will no longer be defined solely by exclusivity and opulence. Instead, it will encompass meaningful experiences, authentic connections, and a commitment to social and environmental responsibility. Brands that recognize and adapt to these changes will thrive in the evolving luxury market.

As we look ahead, the future of luxury holds immense potential for innovation, creativity, and positive change. By embracing new paradigms and prioritizing values that resonate with consumers, luxury brands can navigate the complexities of the modern world while remaining true to their heritage and essence

Chapter 13: The Role of Authenticity in Luxury Brands

Introduction

In an era marked by rapid consumerism and changing market dynamics, authenticity has emerged as a critical factor in the success of luxury brands. As consumers become increasingly discerning and knowledgeable, they seek brands that resonate with their values and deliver genuine experiences. This chapter explores the multifaceted role of authenticity in luxury branding, examining how it influences consumer trust, brand loyalty, and overall market positioning.

1. Defining Authenticity in Luxury

Authenticity encompasses various dimensions, from heritage and craftsmanship to transparency and ethical practices.

- **Heritage and Legacy:** Many luxury brands have rich histories that contribute to their authentic identities. This section discusses how brands leverage their heritage to create narratives that resonate with consumers, emphasizing the importance of storytelling in luxury marketing.

- **Craftsmanship and Quality:** Authenticity in luxury often correlates with superior craftsmanship and quality. This chapter examines how brands maintain high standards in production, ensuring that their products are not only luxurious but also genuine in their creation.

2. The Shift in Consumer Expectations

Modern consumers are increasingly prioritizing authenticity over mere luxury, driving brands to rethink their strategies.

- **Demand for Transparency:** Consumers today are more informed and aware of the ethical implications of their purchases. This section explores the growing demand for transparency in sourcing, production practices, and brand values, highlighting brands that lead the way in ethical luxury.

- **Personal Connections:** Today's consumers seek personal connections with brands that reflect their values and beliefs. This chapter discusses how luxury brands can cultivate meaningful relationships with their audience through genuine communication and engagement.

3. Building Trust Through Authenticity

Trust is a cornerstone of successful luxury branding, and authenticity plays a crucial role in fostering that trust.

- **Brand Consistency:** Authentic luxury brands maintain consistency in their messaging, practices, and values. This section explores the importance of aligning brand promises with actual consumer experiences, ensuring that consumers feel confident in their purchases.

- **Engaging with Criticism:** In an age of social media, brands are under constant scrutiny. This chapter examines how luxury brands can address criticism and challenges while remaining true to their authentic selves, turning potential setbacks into opportunities for growth.

4. The Impact of Social Media on Authenticity

Social media has transformed the luxury landscape, offering both challenges and opportunities for brands striving for authenticity.

- **Real-Time Engagement**: Luxury brands can now engage with consumers in real time, allowing for more genuine interactions. This section discusses how brands can use social media platforms to share authentic stories, behind-the-scenes content, and customer experiences.

- **User-Generated Content**: Consumers increasingly rely on user-generated content to inform their purchasing decisions. This chapter explores the significance of encouraging and curating authentic consumer experiences, showcasing how real customers can enhance a brand's image.

5. Authenticity vs. Exclusivity

Luxury has traditionally been associated with exclusivity, but the modern consumer landscape challenges this notion.

- **Balancing Exclusivity and Accessibility**: Brands must navigate the fine line between maintaining exclusivity and being accessible to a broader audience. This section examines strategies that luxury brands can employ to democratize luxury while preserving authenticity.

- **Creating Inclusive Luxury:** As societal values shift towards inclusivity, luxury brands must adapt. This chapter discusses how embracing diversity and inclusivity can enhance a brand's authenticity, appealing to a wider range of consumers.

6. Case Studies of Authentic Luxury Brands

Several luxury brands exemplify the successful integration of authenticity into their strategies.

- **Hermès:** Known for its commitment to craftsmanship and timelessness, Hermès remains an icon of authentic luxury. This section explores how the brand's dedication to quality and heritage has fostered lasting loyalty among consumers.

- **Patagonia:** While not a traditional luxury brand, Patagonia's commitment to sustainability and ethical practices has positioned it as a leader in the premium market. This chapter discusses how its authenticity-driven approach has resonated with consumers seeking purpose-driven brands.

7. The Future of Authenticity in Luxury

As the luxury landscape evolves, the role of authenticity will continue to shape the industry.

- **Innovation with Integrity:** Luxury brands must innovate while staying true to their authentic values. This section examines how brands can embrace new technologies and trends without compromising their core identity.

- **Consumer-Centric Authenticity**: The future of luxury will depend on brands' ability to adapt to changing consumer expectations. This chapter discusses the importance of listening to consumers and evolving authentically in response to their needs and desires.

Conclusion

Authenticity is no longer an optional trait for luxury brands; it is essential for survival in a competitive and ever-evolving market. By embracing authenticity, luxury brands can foster trust, build lasting relationships with consumers, and differentiate themselves in a crowded marketplace. In a world where consumers seek genuine experiences and values-driven narratives, authenticity will continue to be a guiding principle for successful luxury branding.

Chapter 14: Luxury in the Age of Sustainability

Introduction

As the world grapples with the pressing challenges of climate change, resource depletion, and social inequities, the luxury industry is at a pivotal crossroads. The traditional notions of luxury, often tied to excess and exclusivity, are being reevaluated in favor of more sustainable practices that resonate with the values of modern consumers. This chapter explores how the luxury sector is adapting to the age of sustainability, examining the implications for brands, consumers, and the industry as a whole.

1. Defining Sustainable Luxury

Sustainable luxury is not merely an oxymoron; it represents a new paradigm where luxury is synonymous with ethical practices and environmental responsibility.

- **Conceptualizing Sustainable Luxury:** This section defines what sustainable luxury means in today's context, highlighting the importance of combining luxury with social and environmental consciousness.

- **The Evolving Luxury Consumer:** Modern consumers are increasingly seeking products that reflect their values, prioritizing sustainability alongside quality and craftsmanship. This chapter discusses how brands are responding to this shift in consumer expectations.

2. The Intersection of Luxury and Sustainability

Luxury brands are uniquely positioned to lead the charge towards sustainability, given their influence and resources.

- **Sustainable Sourcing:** Luxury brands are investing in ethically sourced materials, from organic cotton to responsibly mined gemstones. This section explores how brands are ensuring transparency in their supply chains and supporting fair labor practices.

- **Circular Economy:** The concept of a circular economy—where products are designed for longevity, reuse, and recycling—is gaining traction in the luxury sector. This chapter discusses how brands are innovating to reduce waste and extend the lifecycle of their products.

3. The Role of Innovation in Sustainable Luxury

Innovation is key to integrating sustainability into luxury brands, driving change in materials, processes, and consumer engagement.

- **Technological Advancements:** From biodegradable materials to advanced recycling techniques, technology is reshaping the luxury landscape. This section explores how brands are leveraging innovation to create sustainable products without compromising on quality or aesthetics.

- **Design for Sustainability:** This chapter examines how luxury designers are rethinking product design, emphasizing durability and timelessness. The importance of creating products that withstand trends and stand the test of time is highlighted.

4. Communicating Sustainability: Marketing Strategies

Effectively communicating sustainability efforts is crucial for luxury brands to resonate with consumers.

- **Authentic Storytelling:** Brands must engage in genuine storytelling that highlights their commitment to sustainability. This section discusses successful case studies where brands have effectively communicated their sustainability initiatives.

- **Transparency and Accountability:** Consumers expect transparency regarding a brand's sustainability claims. This chapter emphasizes the importance of providing clear and honest information about sourcing, production practices, and environmental impact.

5. The Challenges of Implementing Sustainable Practices

Despite the growing emphasis on sustainability, luxury brands face several challenges in implementing sustainable practices.

- **Balancing Profit and Purpose:** Luxury brands often struggle to balance profitability with sustainable initiatives. This section examines the financial implications of adopting sustainable practices and the long-term benefits that can arise from a commitment to sustainability.

- **Consumer Perception:** There can be scepticism regarding the authenticity of luxury brands' sustainability claims. This chapter discusses the need for brands to build trust and credibility in their sustainability efforts.

6. Case Studies of Sustainable Luxury Brands

Several luxury brands exemplify successful integration of sustainability into their business models.

- **Stella McCartney:** Known for her commitment to sustainable fashion, Stella McCartney has become a leader in the industry by advocating for ethical practices. This section explores how the brand prioritizes sustainability in its sourcing and production processes.

- **Gucci:** With initiatives like Gucci Equilibrium, the brand is focused on sustainability and social responsibility. This chapter examines how Gucci has integrated sustainability into its core strategy while maintaining its luxurious appeal.

7. The Future of Luxury in a Sustainable World

The future of luxury will be shaped by the growing emphasis on sustainability and ethical practices.

- **Consumer-Driven Change:** As consumer awareness increases, brands must adapt to shifting demands. This section discusses the importance of staying attuned to consumer preferences and aligning with their values.

- **Regenerative Practices**: The chapter highlights the emerging trend of regenerative practices, where brands not only aim to reduce harm but actively contribute to the environment and society. This forward-thinking approach represents the next evolution in sustainable luxury.

8. Luxury Beyond Products

Sustainability in luxury extends beyond physical products to encompass experiences, services, and community engagement.

- **Luxury Experiences**: This section explores how luxury brands are creating sustainable experiences that resonate with consumers, from eco-friendly travel options to experiential events that prioritize environmental responsibility.

- **Community and Social Impact**: Luxury brands are increasingly recognizing their role in supporting communities and social initiatives. This chapter discusses how brands can leverage their influence to drive positive change in society.

Conclusion

In the age of sustainability, luxury is undergoing a profound transformation. As brands adapt to the evolving expectations of consumers, they must embrace sustainability as a core principle rather than a mere marketing strategy. By redefining luxury to encompass ethical practices, transparency, and environmental responsibility, the luxury industry can not only thrive but also contribute positively to society and the planet. The future of luxury lies in its ability to align with the values of the modern consumer, creating a new standard for what it means to be truly luxurious in a sustainable world.

Chapter 15: The Psychology of Luxury Shopping

Introduction

The act of purchasing luxury goods is often imbued with complex psychological motivations that extend far beyond mere material desire. Understanding the psychology of luxury shopping reveals how consumers engage with brands, their products, and the broader implications of luxury consumption on identity and self-worth. This chapter explores the various psychological drivers behind luxury shopping, examining how emotions, social influences, and individual aspirations converge in the pursuit of luxury.

1. Understanding Luxury as a Psychological Need

Luxury shopping is not just about acquiring high-end products; it often fulfills deeper psychological needs.

- **The Role of Self-Identity**: Luxury goods serve as a form of self-expression, allowing individuals to project their identity and status. This section explores how consumers curate their image through the brands they choose to associate with.

- **Status and Hierarchy**: Luxury items often signify social status and wealth. This chapter discusses how the desire for status drives individuals to seek out luxury goods as a means of affirming their place within social hierarchies.

2. Emotional Drivers of Luxury Consumption

Emotions play a pivotal role in the decision to engage in luxury shopping.

- **Instant Gratification:** The act of purchasing luxury goods often provides immediate emotional satisfaction. This section explores how luxury shopping acts as a form of escapism, offering temporary relief from stress or dissatisfaction.

- **The Role of Nostalgia:** For many consumers, luxury items can evoke nostalgic feelings, linking them to memories of significant moments or achievements. This chapter examines how nostalgia influences luxury purchases and enhances the emotional value of these items.

3. The Influence of Social Factors

Social influences significantly impact the motivations behind luxury shopping.

- **Peer Pressure and Social Comparison:** The desire to fit in or stand out can drive individuals toward luxury consumption. This section discusses how social media and peer dynamics amplify these pressures, pushing consumers to seek out luxury goods as a way to align with or distinguish themselves from their social circles.

- **Cultural Influences:** Cultural background plays a critical role in shaping attitudes toward luxury. This chapter explores how different cultures perceive luxury, affecting consumers' motivations and justifications for luxury purchases.

4. The Role of Marketing and Brand Image

The marketing strategies employed by luxury brands significantly influence consumer psychology.

- **Aspirational Marketing:** Luxury brands often use aspirational marketing tactics that create a sense of desire and longing. This section examines how the portrayal of an idealized lifestyle in advertising fuels the desire for luxury goods.

- **Brand Storytelling:** The narratives that luxury brands create about their heritage, craftsmanship, and exclusivity resonate with consumers on an emotional level. This chapter discusses how effective storytelling can deepen the psychological connection between consumers and luxury brands.

5. The Impact of Shopping Environment

The shopping environment itself can shape the psychological experience of luxury shopping.

- **Store Ambiance and Design:** The physical space in which luxury goods are sold plays a critical role in influencing consumer emotions and perceptions. This section explores how luxury retailers create immersive shopping experiences that enhance feelings of exclusivity and desire.

- **Customer Service and Personalization:** The level of service and attention provided in luxury retail environments can significantly impact consumer satisfaction and loyalty. This chapter discusses how personalized experiences create emotional bonds with consumers, fostering repeat purchases.

6. The Psychology of Impulse Buying

Luxury shopping often involves impulsive decisions driven by emotional triggers.

- **Emotional Spending:** This section examines how emotions such as happiness, sadness, or stress can lead to impulsive luxury purchases. Understanding the triggers behind impulse buying can provide insights into consumer behavior in the luxury market.

- **Limited Editions and Scarcity:** The concept of scarcity in luxury goods can create a sense of urgency that triggers impulsive buying. This chapter explores how limited editions and exclusive releases play on consumer psychology, driving demand and rapid purchasing decisions.

7. The Consequences of Luxury Shopping

While luxury shopping can fulfil psychological needs, it also carries potential consequences.

- **Guilt and Regret:** After the thrill of the purchase, consumers may experience feelings of guilt or regret, particularly if the purchase strains their finances. This section discusses the psychological aftermath of luxury shopping and its impact on overall well-being.

- **The Cycle of Desire:** The pursuit of luxury can lead to a never-ending cycle of desire, where satisfaction is fleeting, and the craving for more takes hold. This chapter examines how this cycle can contribute to feelings of inadequacy and dissatisfaction.

8. Strategies for Mindful Luxury Shopping

To mitigate negative psychological impacts, consumers can adopt strategies for more mindful luxury shopping.

- **Setting Intentions:** This section emphasizes the importance of setting clear intentions before engaging in luxury shopping, helping consumers differentiate between wants and needs.

- **Fostering Gratitude:** Cultivating a sense of gratitude for what one already possesses can help counteract the constant desire for more. This chapter explores techniques for fostering gratitude in the context of luxury consumption.

Conclusion

The psychology of luxury shopping is a multifaceted landscape shaped by emotional, social, and cultural influences. By understanding the motivations behind luxury consumption, both consumers and brands can navigate the complexities of the luxury market more effectively. As the conversation around sustainability and ethical consumption continues to evolve, recognizing the psychological drivers of luxury shopping will be essential in redefining what it means to indulge in luxury in a responsible and fulfilling manner.

Chapter 16: The Digital Transformation of Luxury

Introduction

The luxury industry is undergoing a profound transformation driven by digital innovation. This chapter examines how technology has reshaped the luxury landscape, impacting marketing strategies, consumer engagement, and the very nature of luxury itself. By understanding the digital transformation, luxury brands can harness these changes to meet evolving consumer expectations and navigate the future of luxury.

1. The Shift from Traditional Retail to E-commerce

The luxury market has historically relied on an exclusive in-store experience, but the rise of e-commerce has revolutionized this model.

- **Growth of Online Luxury Sales**: E-commerce has emerged as a significant channel for luxury sales, particularly during the COVID-19 pandemic. According to reports, online luxury sales grew by over 50% during this period, as consumers shifted to online shopping. This section will delve into specific statistics, providing a detailed analysis of the shift from in-store to online sales and its implications for luxury brands.

- **Challenges and Opportunities**: Transitioning to e-commerce presents both challenges and opportunities. Luxury brands must navigate issues such as maintaining brand integrity and exclusivity in a digital space. This part will explore how luxury brands can strategically approach online sales, balancing accessibility with the desire for exclusivity.

- **Case Studies of Successful E-commerce Strategies**: Highlight successful luxury brands that have embraced e-commerce effectively, such as Gucci and Chanel. Analyse their strategies, focusing on website design, user experience, and customer engagement. For example, Gucci's interactive website features storytelling elements that enhance the online shopping experience.

2. The Role of Social Media

Social media has become an integral part of luxury branding, influencing consumer perceptions and purchasing behaviours.

- **Influencer Marketing**: The rise of social media influencers has transformed how luxury brands connect with consumers. This section will explore how luxury brands collaborate with influencers to create aspirational content and drive engagement. Highlight successful campaigns, such as those by Dior or Louis Vuitton, where influencer partnerships led to increased brand visibility and sales.

- **User-Generated Content**: User-generated content plays a crucial role in building brand loyalty. This section will discuss the importance of encouraging consumers to share their experiences with luxury products on social media. Explore how brands can leverage this content to foster community and enhance their brand image.

- **Social Media Platforms as Marketing Tools**: Analyse how different platforms (Instagram, TikTok, Facebook) serve distinct purposes for luxury brands. For instance, Instagram's visual nature is ideal for showcasing products, while TikTok allows for more interactive engagement. Discuss how brands tailor their content to fit each platform's unique characteristics.

3. Personalization and Data-Driven Marketing

Digital transformation has enabled luxury brands to use data analytics for personalized marketing efforts.

- **Understanding Consumer Behaviour**: Analyse how data analytics helps luxury brands understand consumer preferences and behaviours. Discuss the importance of customer segmentation and how brands can tailor their marketing strategies based on data insights. Use examples of brands that successfully implement data-driven marketing, like Burberry.

- **Personalized Shopping Experiences**: Explore how luxury brands utilize AI and machine learning to provide personalized recommendations and tailored shopping experiences. Discuss the implementation of chatbots and virtual assistants to enhance customer service and engagement. Highlight examples like Net-a-Porter, which uses AI to recommend products based on user behaviour.

- **Building Customer Loyalty through Personalization:** Discuss how personalization fosters brand loyalty. Examine loyalty programs and personalized communication strategies that luxury brands employ to retain customers. Highlight successful examples, such as Sephora's Beauty Insider program, which personalizes offers based on individual preferences.

4. The Rise of Virtual Experiences

As consumers increasingly seek immersive experiences, luxury brands are exploring virtual avenues for engagement.

- **Virtual Reality and Augmented Reality:** Discuss the potential of VR and AR in creating immersive shopping experiences. Highlight case studies of brands using AR technology to allow customers to virtually try on products. For instance, talk about how brands like Warby Parker and L'Oréal are utilizing AR to enhance the consumer experience.

- **Live Streaming and Virtual Events:** Analyse the effectiveness of live streaming for luxury brands to showcase new collections and engage with consumers in real-time. Explore how brands are creating exclusive online events to generate excitement and urgency around product launches, citing examples from brands like Fendi and Gucci.

- **Interactive Brand Experiences:** Discuss how luxury brands create interactive online experiences that resonate with consumers. Explore how brands like Louis Vuitton have implemented online games and quizzes that not only engage but also educate consumers about their heritage and products.

5. Sustainability and Digital Responsibility

With the rise of conscious consumerism, luxury brands must align their digital strategies with sustainability.

- **Transparency and Traceability:** Explore how digital platforms provide opportunities for luxury brands to communicate their sustainability efforts. Discuss how brands can use technology to share information about sourcing, production processes, and ethical practices. Highlight examples of brands like Stella McCartney that have successfully integrated sustainability into their branding.

- **Balancing Luxury with Responsibility:** Analyze the challenges luxury brands face in maintaining exclusivity while being socially responsible. Discuss how technology can help bridge this gap by enabling brands to offer sustainable luxury without compromising on quality or design.

- **Consumer Expectations and Digital Ethics:** Discuss the growing consumer demand for ethical practices and how luxury brands can respond. Explore the importance of ethical marketing, data privacy, and responsible digital practices in maintaining consumer trust.

6. Digital Transformation in Customer Service

Exceptional customer service remains a hallmark of luxury brands, and digital transformation enhances this aspect.

- **Omnichannel Customer Support:** Discuss the importance of providing seamless customer support across various platforms, including online chat, social media, and email. Highlight examples of luxury brands that excel in omnichannel support, such as Hermès, which maintains high-quality customer service across all channels.

- **Chatbots and AI Assistants:** Explore the role of chatbots and AI in providing instant support to consumers. Discuss how luxury brands can implement AI-driven solutions to enhance customer experiences while maintaining the personal touch. Analyze the effectiveness of AI in answering queries and providing personalized recommendations.

- **Building Relationships through Digital Engagement:** Discuss how luxury brands can utilize digital channels to build meaningful relationships with customers. Explore strategies for engaging customers beyond the purchase, such as personalized follow-ups and exclusive offers.

7. The Future of Luxury in a Digital World

As technology continues to evolve, the future of luxury will likely be shaped by emerging trends.

- **Emerging Technologies:** Explore the potential impact of technologies such as blockchain, AI, and the metaverse on the luxury market. Discuss how these innovations can enhance transparency, personalization, and consumer engagement. Consider the implications of the metaverse for luxury brands and how they can create virtual experiences for consumers.

- **Adapting to Changing Consumer Preferences**: Analyse how luxury brands must adapt to the evolving preferences of consumers in a digital age. Discuss the importance of flexibility and innovation in responding to new trends, such as sustainability and digital experiences.

- **Maintaining Human Connection**: Despite the digital shift, the importance of human connection remains vital. Discuss how luxury brands can integrate technology while preserving the personal touch that defines luxury experiences. Explore strategies for creating authentic and meaningful interactions with consumers.

Conclusion

The digital transformation of luxury presents both challenges and opportunities for brands navigating this new landscape. By embracing technology and leveraging digital strategies, luxury brands can connect with consumers in innovative ways while maintaining the values that define luxury. The future of luxury lies in finding a balance between digital innovation and the human touch, ensuring that the essence of luxury continues to resonate in a rapidly changing world.

Chapter 17: Luxury as a Cultural Statement

Introduction

Luxury transcends mere materialism; it embodies cultural narratives and social values. This chapter delves into how luxury goods and experiences serve as cultural statements, reflecting identity, status, and social dynamics. By examining luxury through the lens of culture, we can better understand its significance in contemporary society.

1. Defining Luxury in Cultural Context

- **Cultural Significance of Luxury**: Explore how luxury is defined differently across cultures. In some societies, luxury is synonymous with heritage and craftsmanship, while in others, it may represent modernity and innovation. This section will provide a comparative analysis of luxury perceptions in diverse cultures.

- **Symbolism of Luxury Goods**: Analyse the symbolism attached to luxury items, which often serve as markers of identity and belonging. Discuss how luxury goods can signify social status, wealth, or even cultural heritage. Use examples of cultural artifacts, like traditional clothing or handcrafted jewellery, that embody luxury in various societies.

- **The Evolution of Luxury Standards**: Discuss how luxury standards evolve over time, influenced by cultural shifts, economic factors, and social movements. This section will highlight significant changes in the luxury landscape, particularly in response to globalization and digitalization.

2. Luxury and Identity Formation

    - **Personal Identity through Luxury**: Examine how individuals use luxury goods to express their identity. Discuss how luxury brands provide consumers with a means to showcase their values, aspirations, and social status. Explore the psychological implications of luxury consumption in shaping personal identity.

    - **Group Identity and Luxury Consumption**: Discuss how luxury goods can serve as tools for group identity. Analyse how certain luxury brands create communities around shared values or lifestyles, reinforcing a sense of belonging among consumers. Highlight examples like membership clubs and exclusive brand communities.

    - **Cultural Appropriation vs. Appreciation**: Explore the complex dynamics of cultural appropriation in the luxury sector. Discuss how luxury brands often draw inspiration from various cultures and the ethical considerations surrounding this practice. Highlight case studies where cultural elements have been incorporated into luxury branding, prompting discussions on authenticity and respect.

3. **Luxury in Globalization**
   - **Global vs. Local Luxury:** Analyse the impact of globalization on luxury consumption. Discuss how luxury brands have adapted to local cultures while maintaining their global identity. Explore the balance between global branding strategies and local cultural nuances.
   - **Emerging Markets and New Cultural Narratives:** Examine how emerging markets, particularly in Asia and Africa, are reshaping the luxury narrative. Discuss how local traditions and values influence luxury consumption patterns in these regions. Use examples of brands that have successfully localized their offerings to resonate with new markets.
   - **Cultural Hybridization in Luxury:** Explore the phenomenon of cultural hybridization, where luxury brands blend elements from various cultures to create unique products. Discuss how this approach can appeal to a global audience while respecting cultural heritage. Highlight successful brands that embody this concept.

4. **Luxury as a Reflection of Social Dynamics**
   - **Status Symbols and Social Hierarchies:** Discuss how luxury goods often serve as status symbols, reinforcing social hierarchies. Analyse the role of conspicuous consumption in signalling wealth and privilege. Explore how luxury brands position themselves within these dynamics.

- **Cultural Shifts and Social Movements:** Examine how social movements, such as sustainability and inclusivity, influence luxury consumption. Discuss how luxury brands are responding to changing societal values and the implications for their cultural relevance. Highlight brands that have embraced social responsibility as part of their identity.

- **Luxury and Economic Disparity:** Analyse the relationship between luxury consumption and economic disparity. Discuss how the perception of luxury can perpetuate social inequality and the ethical considerations surrounding this issue. Explore how luxury brands navigate these challenges in their marketing strategies.

5. The Role of Art and Culture in Luxury

- **Luxury and Artistic Expression:** Explore the connection between luxury and the arts. Discuss how luxury brands collaborate with artists, designers, and creatives to produce limited-edition collections. Highlight case studies of successful collaborations that have elevated both the brand and the artist.

- **Cultural Events and Luxury Experiences:** Discuss how luxury brands sponsor and participate in cultural events, such as art exhibitions, film festivals, and music events. Analyse the role of experiential marketing in enhancing brand prestige and cultural relevance.

- **Storytelling and Cultural Narratives:** Examine the importance of storytelling in luxury branding. Discuss how brands use narratives to connect with consumers emotionally and culturally. Highlight examples of brands that have successfully crafted compelling stories around their heritage and values.

6. Future Trends: Luxury in a Cultural Context

- **The Impact of Technology on Cultural Luxury:** Discuss how emerging technologies, such as virtual reality and augmented reality, are changing the way consumers experience luxury. Explore how technology can enhance cultural storytelling and provide immersive experiences for consumers.

- **Sustainability and Cultural Consciousness:** Analyse the growing importance of sustainability in luxury consumption. Discuss how consumers are increasingly seeking luxury brands that align with their values and cultural beliefs. Explore how brands can innovate sustainably while preserving their cultural narratives.

- **The Role of Diversity and Inclusion:** Examine the increasing demand for diversity and inclusion within the luxury industry. Discuss how luxury brands are responding to calls for representation and authenticity in their marketing strategies. Highlight brands that are leading the way in promoting cultural diversity.

Conclusion

Luxury serves as a powerful cultural statement, reflecting societal values, aspirations, and identities. As the luxury landscape continues to evolve, brands must navigate the complexities of cultural dynamics while remaining authentic and responsible. By understanding the cultural implications of luxury, brands can create meaningful connections with consumers and ensure their relevance in a rapidly changing world.

Chapter 18: Navigating the Luxury Market Post-Pandemic

Introduction

The COVID-19 pandemic has profoundly impacted consumer behaviour and the luxury market. As the world adapts to a new normal, luxury brands must navigate the challenges and opportunities that have emerged in the wake of the pandemic. This chapter explores the shifts in consumer expectations, market dynamics, and strategic adaptations within the luxury industry in the post-pandemic era.

1. The Immediate Impact of the Pandemic on Luxury Consumption

- **Decline in Sales and Market Disruption:** Discuss how the pandemic led to a significant decline in luxury sales globally. Analyze the factors contributing to this downturn, including store closures, travel restrictions, and changes in consumer priorities. Use data and statistics to illustrate the extent of the impact.

- **Shift in Consumer Priorities:** Explore how consumer priorities shifted during the pandemic, with an increased focus on health, safety, and essential needs. Discuss how this shift affected spending patterns, leading to a temporary decline in luxury purchases.

- **Adapting to New Norms:** Highlight how luxury brands adapted to the immediate challenges of the pandemic, such as enhancing online shopping experiences and implementing safety protocols in physical stores. Provide examples of brands that successfully pivoted their strategies during this period.

2. The Rise of Digital and E-Commerce

- **Acceleration of Digital Transformation**: Analyse how the pandemic accelerated the digital transformation of the luxury market. Discuss the rise of e-commerce and online luxury shopping, emphasizing how brands invested in their digital infrastructure to meet changing consumer demands.

- **Virtual Experiences and Engagement**: Explore how luxury brands developed virtual experiences to engage consumers during lockdowns. Discuss the use of virtual showrooms, live-streaming events, and social media campaigns to connect with audiences in innovative ways.

- **Omni-Channel Retail Strategies**: Examine the importance of adopting omni-channel retail strategies in the post-pandemic luxury market. Discuss how brands can create seamless shopping experiences across online and offline channels, enhancing customer satisfaction and loyalty.

3. Shifts in Consumer Behaviour and Expectations

- **Emphasis on Wellness and Sustainability**: Discuss the growing consumer emphasis on wellness and sustainability in luxury consumption. Analyse how consumers are increasingly seeking brands that align with their values, particularly regarding health and environmental responsibility.

- **Experience over Materialism:** Explore the trend of consumers prioritizing experiences over material possessions post-pandemic. Discuss how luxury brands can cater to this shift by offering unique experiences, personalized services, and immersive brand interactions.

- **Reevaluating Luxury Definitions:** Examine how the pandemic prompted consumers to reevaluate their definitions of luxury. Discuss how luxury is increasingly viewed as a holistic concept, encompassing quality of life, well-being, and emotional satisfaction.

4. The Role of Authenticity and Transparency

- **Demand for Authenticity:** Analyse the heightened demand for authenticity in the luxury market post-pandemic. Discuss how consumers are seeking genuine connections with brands and transparency in sourcing, production, and business practices.

- **Building Trust and Loyalty:** Explore how luxury brands can build trust and loyalty by embracing transparency and ethical practices. Highlight case studies of brands that have successfully communicated their values and engaged consumers authentically.

- **Emphasizing Heritage and Craftsmanship:** Discuss the resurgence of interest in heritage and craftsmanship in the luxury sector. Explore how consumers are drawn to brands that emphasize their history, tradition, and artisanal production methods.

5. **Reimagining Luxury Marketing Strategies**

    - **Personalization and Customer Experience:** Discuss the importance of personalization in luxury marketing strategies. Analyze how brands can leverage data and technology to create tailored experiences that resonate with individual consumers.

    - **Collaborations and Partnerships:** Explore the potential for collaborations and partnerships within the luxury market. Discuss how brands can leverage cross-industry collaborations to create unique offerings and engage diverse consumer segments.

    - **Social Media and Influencer Marketing:** Examine the evolving role of social media and influencer marketing in the luxury sector. Discuss how brands can effectively use these platforms to reach and engage their target audiences in an authentic manner.

6. **The Future of Luxury in a Post-Pandemic World**

    - **Emerging Trends and Opportunities:** Discuss the emerging trends and opportunities in the luxury market as the world recovers from the pandemic. Analyse how brands can adapt to changing consumer preferences and navigate the evolving market landscape.

- **Resilience and Adaptability:** Explore the importance of resilience and adaptability in the luxury sector. Discuss how brands can remain agile and responsive to market changes, leveraging innovation and creativity to stay relevant.

- **Sustainable Growth and Responsible Practices:** Emphasize the importance of sustainable growth and responsible practices in the future of luxury. Discuss how brands can align their strategies with consumer expectations for social and environmental responsibility.

Conclusion

The post-pandemic luxury market presents both challenges and opportunities for brands navigating this new landscape. By embracing digital transformation, authenticity, and evolving consumer expectations, luxury brands can thrive in a world reshaped by the pandemic. As they adapt to these changes, the luxury sector can redefine its role in society, fostering meaningful connections with consumers while promoting sustainability and responsible practices.

Chapter 19: The Intersection of Technology and Luxury

Introduction

The luxury industry has long been associated with timelessness, craftsmanship, and exclusivity. However, in an era defined by rapid technological advancement, luxury brands are increasingly embracing innovation to enhance consumer experiences, streamline operations, and redefine their value propositions. This chapter explores the intersection of technology and luxury, examining how brands are leveraging technological advancements to stay relevant in a rapidly changing market.

1. The Digital Transformation of Luxury Brands

- **Embracing E-Commerce**: Discuss the shift from traditional retail to e-commerce within the luxury sector. Highlight how brands have developed sophisticated online platforms to cater to the growing demand for digital shopping experiences. Provide examples of luxury brands that have successfully transitioned to online sales while maintaining their brand identity.

- **Creating Immersive Online Experiences**: Explore how luxury brands are using technology to create immersive online shopping experiences. Discuss innovations such as virtual reality (VR) and augmented reality (AR) that allow consumers to visualize products in real-time and try them virtually.

- **The Role of Data Analytics**: Analyse how luxury brands are utilizing data analytics to understand consumer behaviour better and personalize marketing efforts. Discuss the importance of gathering data on customer preferences, purchase history, and browsing behaviour to create tailored shopping experiences.

2. The Influence of Social Media and Influencer Marketing

- **Social Media as a Marketing Tool**: Examine the significant role of social media in promoting luxury brands. Discuss how platforms like Instagram, TikTok, and Pinterest have transformed the way luxury brands communicate with consumers, showcasing products in aspirational contexts.

- **The Rise of Influencer Culture**: Explore the impact of influencer marketing on luxury consumption. Discuss how luxury brands collaborate with influencers to reach younger audiences and create authentic connections. Highlight case studies of successful influencer partnerships that have elevated brand visibility.

- **User-Generated Content and Brand Engagement**: Analyse the importance of user-generated content in the luxury sector. Discuss how luxury brands encourage consumers to share their experiences and showcase products on social media, fostering community engagement and brand loyalty.

3. Enhancing Customer Experience with Technology

- **Personalization and Customization:** Discuss how technology enables luxury brands to offer personalized and customizable products. Explore the use of online configurators and bespoke services that allow consumers to tailor products to their preferences, enhancing the luxury experience.

- **Chatbots and AI-Driven Customer Service:** Examine the integration of artificial intelligence (AI) in customer service. Discuss how luxury brands are using chatbots and AI-driven solutions to provide 24/7 support, answer queries, and assist consumers in their shopping journeys.

- **Omni-Channel Retailing:** Analyse the significance of omni-channel retail strategies in the luxury market. Discuss how technology allows brands to create seamless shopping experiences across online and offline channels, enabling consumers to transition between platforms effortlessly.

4. Blockchain Technology and Authenticity

- **Ensuring Product Authenticity:** Explore the role of blockchain technology in combating counterfeiting and ensuring product authenticity in the luxury market. Discuss how brands can utilize blockchain to provide transparent supply chain information, allowing consumers to verify the authenticity and provenance of luxury items.

- **Smart Contracts and Ownership Tracking**: Discuss how smart contracts on blockchain can facilitate ownership tracking and resale value for luxury goods. Explore how this technology empowers consumers and brands, fostering trust in the marketplace.

- **Luxury NFTs and Digital Ownership**: Analyse the rise of non-fungible tokens (NFTs) in the luxury sector. Discuss how luxury brands are creating digital assets that represent exclusive items, offering consumers new forms of ownership and engagement.

5. **Sustainability through Technology**

    - **Tech-Driven Sustainable Practices**: Explore how luxury brands are leveraging technology to implement sustainable practices. Discuss innovations in materials sourcing, production processes, and waste management that promote environmental responsibility.

    - **Transparency and Traceability**: Analyse the importance of transparency in luxury consumption. Discuss how technology can provide consumers with insights into a brand's sustainability efforts, allowing them to make informed choices aligned with their values.

    - **Innovative Materials and Circular Economy**: Examine the use of innovative materials, such as lab-grown leather and recycled fabrics, in luxury fashion. Discuss how technology can support the transition to a circular economy, where luxury goods are designed for longevity and recyclability.

6. The Future of Luxury and Technology

- **Embracing Innovation**: Discuss the necessity for luxury brands to embrace innovation to remain competitive in a technology-driven market. Explore how brands can foster a culture of creativity and agility to adapt to emerging trends.

- **Challenges and Considerations**: Analyse the potential challenges luxury brands face in integrating technology. Discuss concerns related to brand identity, maintaining exclusivity, and navigating consumer privacy in an increasingly digital landscape.

- **Vision for the Future**: Provide insights into the future of the luxury industry as it continues to intersect with technology. Discuss potential advancements and how brands can leverage technology to create meaningful connections with consumers while staying true to their heritage.

Conclusion

The intersection of technology and luxury presents both challenges and opportunities for brands navigating an evolving marketplace. By embracing digital transformation, enhancing customer experiences, and prioritizing sustainability, luxury brands can redefine their value propositions and build lasting connections with consumers. As the luxury sector continues to adapt to technological advancements, the future promises a new era of innovation and creativity that reshapes the essence of luxury.

Chapter 20: Creating a Balanced Luxury Lifestyle

Introduction

In a world where luxury often symbolizes success, status, and happiness, it's essential to consider what it means to lead a balanced luxury lifestyle. This chapter delves into the complexities of luxury living, advocating for a harmonious approach that integrates values, well-being, and mindful consumption. We explore how individuals can embrace luxury in a way that enriches their lives without falling into the traps of excess, comparison, and unsustainable practices.

1. Defining a Balanced Luxury Lifestyle

- **What is a Balanced Luxury Lifestyle?** Define the concept of a balanced luxury lifestyle as one that harmonizes indulgence with practicality. Discuss how this lifestyle prioritizes well-being, personal values, and sustainable practices alongside the appreciation of luxury.

- **Luxury vs. Excess:** Examine the difference between luxury and excess. Discuss how the pursuit of luxury can sometimes lead to an unhealthy obsession with material possessions, and how balance can help individuals differentiate between true luxury and mere consumerism.

- **Personal Values and Luxury:** Explore the importance of aligning luxury choices with personal values. Discuss how understanding one's values can guide decisions regarding luxury consumption, ensuring that purchases reflect authenticity and meaningful experiences.

2. Mindful Consumption in Luxury

- **The Philosophy of Minimalism:** Discuss how minimalism can contribute to a balanced luxury lifestyle. Explore the idea that less can be more, focusing on quality over quantity and the emotional benefits of decluttering one's life.

- **Choosing Meaningful Experiences:** Emphasize the value of investing in experiences rather than material possessions. Discuss how travel, cultural events, and personal development can provide lasting joy and fulfilment that material goods cannot.

- **Sustainable Luxury Choices:** Highlight the importance of making sustainable luxury choices. Discuss how opting for eco-friendly brands, ethically sourced materials, and fair-trade practices can contribute to a balanced lifestyle that supports the planet and its people.

3. Cultivating Well-Being through Luxury

- **Self-Care and Luxury:** Explore the relationship between luxury and self-care. Discuss how luxury can be redefined as the time and resources spent on one's well-being, including wellness retreats, spa treatments, and mental health practices.

- **Creating a Luxurious Home Environment:** Discuss how to create a balanced, luxurious home that fosters comfort and relaxation. Highlight design principles that promote tranquillity and well-being, such as incorporating natural elements, minimizing clutter, and investing in quality furnishings.

- **Luxury in Leisure Time:** Explore how individuals can incorporate luxury into their leisure time. Discuss the importance of balancing work with relaxation and pursuing hobbies that bring joy and fulfilment, whether it be gourmet cooking, gardening, or artistic pursuits.

4. Building Meaningful Relationships

- **Quality Over Quantity in Social Connections:** Discuss the importance of nurturing quality relationships over the pursuit of a large social circle. Explore how genuine connections with friends and family contribute to a fulfilling luxury lifestyle.

- **The Role of Community:** Highlight the significance of community in creating a balanced luxury lifestyle. Discuss how engaging with local initiatives, supporting artisans, and participating in social causes can enrich one's life and promote a sense of belonging.

- **Luxury and Emotional Wealth:** Explore the idea that true luxury extends beyond material wealth to include emotional and social wealth. Discuss how prioritizing emotional health and interpersonal relationships contributes to a well-rounded lifestyle.

5. Financial Wellness and Responsible Luxury

- **Setting Financial Boundaries:** Emphasize the importance of setting financial boundaries in luxury consumption. Discuss how creating a budget that reflects one's values can lead to more intentional spending and a balanced approach to luxury.

- **Investing in Quality:** Explore the philosophy of investing in quality over quantity. Discuss how purchasing timeless, high-quality items can lead to long-term satisfaction and reduce the cycle of constant consumption.

- **The Impact of Financial Stress:** Analyse the impact of financial stress on one's ability to enjoy a luxury lifestyle. Discuss how maintaining financial wellness is crucial for achieving a sense of balance and fulfilment.

6. The Future of Balanced Luxury Living

- **Evolving Definitions of Luxury:** Discuss how the definition of luxury is evolving in contemporary society. Highlight the shift towards experiences, sustainability, and wellness, and how these factors shape the future of luxury living.

- **Integrating Technology Mindfully:** Explore how technology can play a role in enhancing a balanced luxury lifestyle. Discuss tools and apps that promote mindfulness, budgeting, and conscious consumption, helping individuals navigate their luxury choices effectively.

- **Encouraging a Collective Shift:** Highlight the importance of encouraging a collective shift toward balanced luxury living within society. Discuss how individuals can advocate for responsible consumption and support brands that prioritize sustainability and ethics.

Conclusion

Creating a balanced luxury lifestyle requires intentionality, mindfulness, and a deep understanding of one's values. By focusing on meaningful experiences, nurturing relationships, and prioritizing well-being, individuals can enjoy the benefits of luxury without falling into the traps of excess and superficiality. As the definition of luxury continues to evolve, embracing a balanced approach will empower individuals to live enriched lives filled with authenticity, purpose, and joy.

Conclusion: Finding Balance in a World Obsessed with More

Introduction

As we navigate a world increasingly obsessed with materialism, success, and the allure of luxury, the need for balance has never been more critical. This concluding chapter synthesizes the insights gleaned throughout the book, emphasizing the importance of redefining our relationship with luxury and adopting a mindset that prioritizes well-being, authenticity, and sustainability.

1. The Paradox of Luxury in Modern Society

- **Luxury as a Double-Edged Sword**: Reflect on how luxury can simultaneously offer comfort and aspiration while also leading to stress, anxiety, and discontent. Discuss the paradox of seeking fulfilment through material possessions while risking a deeper sense of emptiness.

- **Cultural Narratives and Consumerism**: Examine the cultural narratives that glorify consumption and the status associated with luxury goods. Discuss how these narratives shape individual behaviours and societal norms, often at the expense of personal well-being and communal values.

- **The Emotional Toll of FOMO**: Reiterate the emotional toll that fear of missing out (FOMO) can exert on individuals, leading to compulsive consumption and unhealthy comparisons. Emphasize the importance of recognizing these feelings and re-evaluating the motivations behind luxury consumption.

2. Embracing Mindfulness in Luxury Choices

- **The Power of Mindfulness**: Highlight the transformative power of mindfulness in luxury consumption. Discuss how being present and aware of one's choices can lead to more meaningful experiences and reduce the impulse to conform to societal pressures.

- **Intentional Consumption**: Advocate for a shift towards intentional consumption, where purchases are made thoughtfully and align with personal values. Explore strategies for cultivating intentionality, such as creating wish lists, reflecting on motivations, and assessing the long-term value of luxury items.

- **Practicing Gratitude**: Emphasize the role of gratitude in fostering a balanced relationship with luxury. Discuss how practicing gratitude can shift focus from what is lacking to appreciating what one already has, thereby reducing the desire for more.

3. Redefining Success Beyond Material Wealth

- **Success as a Multifaceted Concept:** Discuss the need to redefine success in broader terms that encompass emotional fulfilment, personal growth, and community engagement. Challenge the traditional notion that equates success with wealth and possessions.

- **Setting Personal Goals:** Encourage readers to set personal goals that prioritize well-being and self-improvement over material achievements. Discuss the importance of aligning goals with values and passions to foster a more fulfilling and balanced life.

- **Celebrating Non-Material Achievements:** Advocate for the celebration of non-material achievements, such as personal growth, relationship building, and community contributions. Discuss how recognizing and valuing these aspects can lead to a more enriched life.

4. Sustainability as a Core Principle

- **The Necessity of Sustainable Practices:** Reiterate the urgent need for sustainable practices in luxury consumption. Discuss the environmental and social implications of consumer choices and the role individuals can play in fostering a more sustainable future.

- **Support for Ethical Brands:** Encourage readers to support brands that prioritize ethics and sustainability. Discuss how making conscious choices can influence the market and promote a culture of responsible luxury.

- **The Role of Community and Collaboration:** Emphasize the importance of community and collaboration in driving sustainable practices. Highlight examples of collective efforts that foster responsible consumption and advocate for change within the luxury sector.

5. The Future of Luxury: A Call for Balance

- **Evolving Definitions of Luxury:** Reflect on how the definition of luxury is evolving, particularly in light of societal shifts towards sustainability and well-being. Discuss the potential for a future where luxury embodies authenticity, purpose, and positive impact.

- **A Collective Shift Towards Balance:** Advocate for a collective shift towards balance in luxury consumption. Encourage readers to engage in conversations about responsible consumption and support initiatives that promote a balanced approach to luxury.

- **Empowering Future Generations:** Emphasize the importance of educating future generations about balanced luxury living. Discuss how instilling values of mindfulness, sustainability, and authenticity can create a lasting impact on societal norms.

6. Conclusion: A Journey Towards Balance

- **A Personal Reflection:** Invite readers to reflect on their own relationships with luxury and consumption. Encourage them to assess their values, motivations, and goals, fostering a deeper understanding of what a balanced luxury lifestyle means for them.

- **Embracing the Journey:** Acknowledge that finding balance is an ongoing journey rather than a destination. Encourage readers to embrace the process of self-discovery and growth, understanding that it's okay to adjust their paths as they learn and evolve.

- **A Vision for a Balanced Future:** End with a vision for a future where luxury coexists harmoniously with well-being, sustainability, and authenticity. Inspire readers to contribute to this vision through their choices and actions, cultivating a world where luxury is redefined and balanced.

www.ingramcontent.com/pod-product-compliance
Lightning Source LLC
Chambersburg PA
CBHW050307230526
45471CB00005B/2064